STUDENT-CENTERED SOCIAL STUDIES PROJECTS

Written
by
Michael Koren

Cover & Inside Illustrations
by
Elizabeth Adams

Publisher
Instructional Fair · TS Denison
Grand Rapids, Michigan 49544

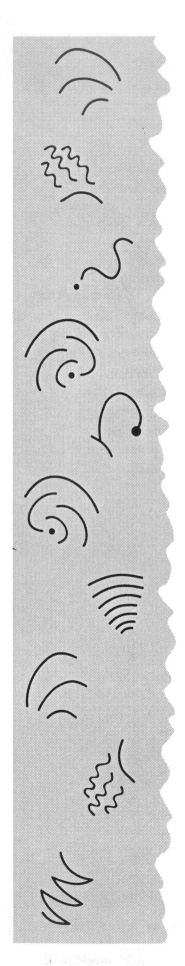

Permission to Reproduce

About the Author

Michael Koren has been a classroom teacher for more than 18 years in Fox Point, Wisconsin. He has earned several degrees from the University of Wisconsin–Milwaukee. They include a Bachelor of Science in Social Studies with a major in history and a minor in economics. He holds masters' degrees in the areas of curriculum and instruction. Michael has given numerous presentations at conferences of the Wisconsin Council for the Social Studies. He has also presented at conventions of the National Council for the Social Studies.

Credits

Author: Michael Koren
Artist: Elizabeth Adams
Cover Graphics: Peggy Jackson
Text Designer: Pat Geasler
Project Director/Editor: Sharon Kirkwood
Editors: Lisa Hancock, Elizabeth Flikkema

Standard Book Number: 1-56822-853-8
Social Studies Projects
Copyright © 1999 by Ideal · Instructional Fair Publishing Group
a division of Tribune Education
2400 Turner Avenue NW
Grand Rapids, Michigan 49544

CURR
H
62
.K67
1999

Table of Contents

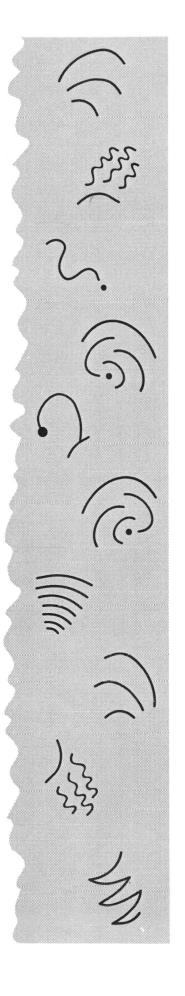

Introduction

This book contains units that are highly interactive and student-centered in nature. I decided to write this book because of the great teacher interest in presentations at local or national conferences on topics dealing with games or highly active social studies lessons. For my own presentations, the demand for handouts always exceeded supplies. Further, the feedback from teachers who had tried these activities, was very positive. Finally, students have told me these lessons are among the most memorable of their school experience.

This book is supplemental in nature. Each teacher should look at his or her own curriculum to see where these lessons might fit. For example, the first several lessons deal with economic concepts. While these lessons would certainly work in an economics classroom, a teacher of history could use the unit dealing with unions while studying the Industrial Revolution. While the lessons nicely fit into a high school economics and/or history curriculum, the concepts are easily adaptable for the middle school.

Teachers should feel free to modify the units to meet their individual classroom needs. For some grade levels, you may wish to substitute other materials for those suggested in the lesson.

I hope you enjoy this book and find it useful in your classroom.

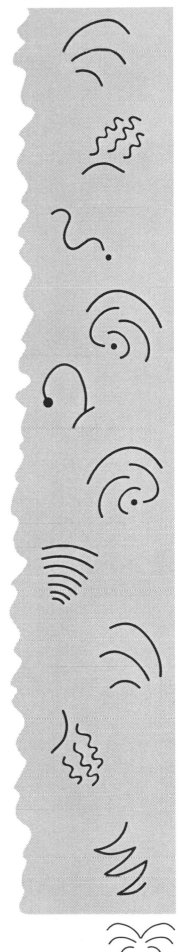

Scarcity and Opportunity Cost

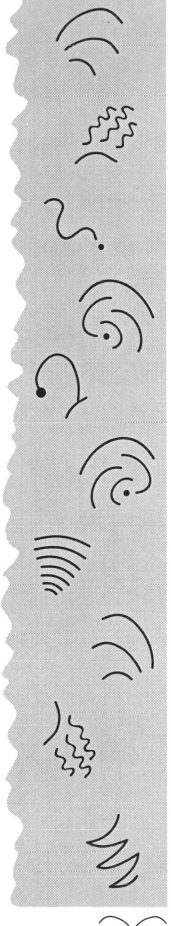

Time

One to two class periods.

Purpose

To enable students to become familiar with the concept of scarcity and opportunity cost; how it affects their lives; and how to deal with it.

Objectives

Students will be able to . . .

- identify scarce resources.
- recognize opportunity cost.
- act upon examples of scarcity.
- explain how scarcity affects their lives.

Vocabulary

scarcity   personal scarcity
opportunity cost   community scarcity
choices

Concepts

- Scarcity and opportunity cost always exist. Individuals, as well as society, must deal with these concepts. Even the wealthiest person in the world must deal with scarcity in the form of a limited amount of time.

- Choices are made based on a range of individual factors. Different people, given the same set of circumstances, may make completely different choices. Likewise, societies and communities will make different choices from one another based on their own set of variables.

1. Present the concept of scarcity.

   • Ask students to write a list of three to five things they would like to have. These could be material or nonmaterial.

   • Ask students to write next to each item why they are unable to have that item.

   Note: Having students do this silently and having them write why they can't have the things on their lists tends to keep students focused and serious about what they are doing.

2. Ask students to define scarcity. One definition is ***unlimited desires which cannot be fulfilled due to limited resources.***

   Discuss the differences between personal and community scarcity.

   • Personal scarcity occurs when a person wants something but can't have it because of a lack of resources.

   • Community scarcity occurs when a community wants something but can't have it because of a lack of resources.

     Examples: access to medical care, good schools, curbside garbage collection, and well-paved streets.

3. Propose some scenarios involving scarce resources. Have students identify the scarce resource, the decision that they must make, and what they give up.

   Example: Bradley wants to see a movie and buy a box of candy for his dad's birthday. However, he has only $5.00, and each item costs $5.00.

4. Ask students to define opportunity cost. One definition is **things a person cannot have because of a decision to use a limited resource in another way.**

5. Make copies of and discuss the worksheet, "Choices," on page 11. As a class, read each situation, and have students identify the opportunity cost involved with each situation.

6. Make copies of and have students complete the worksheet, "Scarcity Scenarios," on page 12. Discuss each situation when students finish.

   • To save time, students could work in groups. Assign each group to one or two situations.

   • To illustrate that scarcity may not always be a pleasant situation, play the role of an unhappy customer in situation B and an unhappy taxpayer in situation C. No matter what solution the students propose, you will not be happy. Making choices may cause some people to be unhappy.

7. Make copies of the "Scarcity Log" on page 13. After seven days, have students share some of their situations regarding scarcity.

8. Play the $5,000 Lottery game.

   • Give each student a copy of the "$5,000 Lottery" handout on page 14. Each student should spend as mush as possible of the $5,000 and put any money not spent in a savings account.

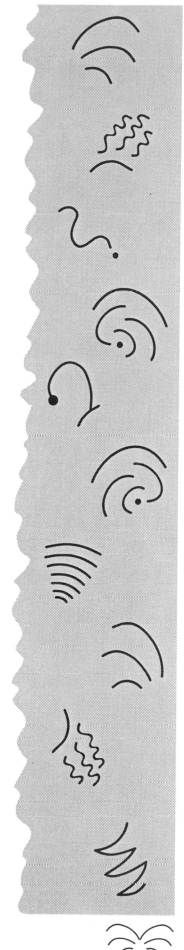

- After students have completed their handout, give them a second copy of the same handout. This one is for their parents to complete at home.

- After the parents have completed the worksheet, the students should compare their work with that of their parents. Parents and students should discuss the results of their efforts. It is important that parents and students talk about why there are similarities and differences in spending patterns.

- The next day in class, students may share information with the class. Discuss the differences found between student and parent. It may indicate that the parent generally considers the whole family, while the student tends to think of him/herself.

9. Review the main ideas of the unit.

〜 Choices 〜

Read each situation below, make a choice, and then identify the opportunity cost involved.

Situation 1

You have earned $80.00 doing yard work. You have several possible ways to spend the money, but you must have at least $50.00 left over to put into savings.

Your choices are:
- Go to dinner with friends $10.00
- Buy school supplies $14.00
- Buy soda and snacks for a party $17.00
- Buy some gas for your car $12.00

What would you do choose? Explain your choices.
What is the opportunity cost?

Situation 2

You babysit for a neighbor 3 days a week after school for 3 hours each day. You are paid $30.00. You have an opportunity to become a volunteer at a daycare center for 2 hours every day after school. You will have to give up your after-school job to do this, but you expect volunteering will lead to a paid daycare position during the summer at a higher rate of pay and with more hours than you currently receive.

What choice would you make? Explain your choice.
What is the opportunity cost?

Situation 3

You spend 4 days a week tutoring a student. You receive $15.00 for each day you work with this student. This week you have an opportunity to go on vacation with your family.

What decision would you make? Explain your choice.
What is the opportunity cost?

Scarcity Scenarios

Read each situation below and then answer the questions at the bottom of the page.

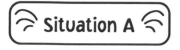
Situation A

Working different jobs, you have managed to save $125.00. You would like to buy concert tickets and CDs, but you are also in need of new shoes, new jeans, and a new shirt. The $125.00 will cover either the concert tickets and CDs, or the shoes, pants, and shirt. You don't have enough money to buy everything.

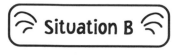
Situation B

You are the postmaster of the local post office. You employ seven people at the post office. Five people are working the sales windows selling stamps, handling special mail requests, and taking care of other sales responsibilities. Two mailcarriers are in the back sorting mail to deliver later that day. An unusually large number of customers have come to the post office to buy stamps, creating long lines.

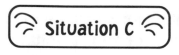
Situation C

You are the mayor of a city of 25,000 people. You have enough maintenance workers to handle three water main breaks at one time. Unfortunately, five breaks occur at the same time. On-call independent maintenance workers are available but their rates exceed the city's budget for maintenance.

Questions

On a separate sheet of paper, complete the following for each situation described above.

1. Identify the limited resource in each situation.

2. What options exist regarding the use of the limited resource for each situation?

3. Identify the opportunity cost(s) for the choice(s) you make for each situation.

© Instructional Fair • TS Denison   IF19311 *Social Studies Projects*

 Scarcity Log

For the next week, keep track of situations in your life where scarcity exists. Write them in the space below. Then tell how you will resolve each situation.

Scarcity Situations	Resolutions

$5,000 Lottery

You have just won $5,000 after taxes in the state lottery. You have an opportunity to decide what to do with the money. Using the items and amounts listed, write how you would spend the money. For your own ideas, you will need to estimate the cost. If there is any money left over, it should be put into a savings account.

Possible Ways to Spend the Money

- $1,000 to start a college fund savings account
- $350 for a new pet
- $400 for a dishwasher
- $2,000 for braces
- $2,400 to buy a used car
- $1,400 for a new computer
- $700 for a new bike

- $2,000 for remodeling a portion of the house
- $400 for a family camping trip
- $800 for new clothes
- $1,500 for some new furniture
- $400 for a summer sports or music camp
- Your own ideas

Spending Chart

Your Choices	Cost of Your Choices
1.	
2.	
3.	
4.	
5.	
6.	
Total Cost =	

IF19311 *Social Studies Projects*

Notes

_____

_____

_____

_____

_____

_____

_____

_____

_____

_____

_____

_____

_____

_____

_____

_____

_____

_____

_____

_____

_____

_____

_____

Supply and Demand

Time

Two to three class periods.

Purpose

To enable students to understand how the principles of supply and demand operate in our economy.

Objectives

Students will be able to . . .

- explain how the laws of supply and demand work.

- explain how supply and demand affects prices.

- give examples of supply and demand principles.

Vocabulary

supply	market price
demand	shortage
inelastic demand	surplus
market supply	

Concepts

- Demand is usually sensitive to price fluctuations. Higher prices usually mean fewer consumers buy. Lower prices usually lead to higher demand.

- Inelastic demand refers to items that people will buy regardless of the price.

- Supply is also price sensitive. When a product sells for a higher price, the supplier has more incentive to produce. The lower the price, the less incentive to provide a product.

- Market price and market supply are determined by where the supply and demand curves intersect.

- Surplus is too much supply, while shortage is too little supply.

1. Distribute copies of the "Demand Worksheet" on page 21 to all students.

   - Ask students to complete the worksheet.

   - Discuss what happens as prices increase.
     The amount demanded should drop.

   - Define demand as **the amount people are ready to buy at a given price.**

   - Discuss inelastic demand. This refers to products for which **price will not have a great influence on demand.** (Gasoline, medical services, heat, and water are some examples.)

2. Distribute copies of the "Supply Worksheet" on page 22.

   - Organize students into groups of three.

   - Tell students they will function as if their group is the only group in the school selling pizza.

   - The group must determine how many pizzas to make and for how much to sell each slice.

   - Ask students what will happen as prices go up. **The amount supplied should go up, since chances for profits are greater. However, if you are not able to sell all you produce, then you have a surplus. This would result in lower profits.** This concept can be pointed out again when students work on "Linda's Fundraiser" on page 23.

A profit will occur at any price over 50¢ per slice. None should be sold at 50¢ or lower, since students will only break even at this point or incur a loss. (Remember, it costs 50¢ to make each slice of pizza.)

- Provide a definition of supply such as *the amount provided at a given price.*

- As an alternate example of a supply activity, see the "Cookie Dough Fundraiser" activity sheet on page 27.

3. For now, present the concepts of market supply and market demand by distributing copies of "Linda's Fundraiser" worksheet on page 23. Have four students read it aloud in class.

- Plot the supply and demand curves on the "Market Price and Supply" graph (page 24).

- Illustrate how price and quantity are determined. *(The price and quantity are determined by finding where the supply and demand curves intersect. Then go to each axis of the graph to find the price and the quantity produced.)*

- Indicate where surplus (too much supply) and shortage (not enough supply) points are on the graph. *(Surplus is any point above the intersection of the two curves. Shortage is any point below the intersection.)*

- Show how profit is not maximized unless supply equals demand. For example, at 50¢, Linda would make $2.50 (50¢ x 5 candy bars sold); at 80¢, she would make $1.60 (80¢ x 2 candy bars sold); at 40¢, Linda would make $2.40, but since Linda would supply only four, she could only make $1.60. **Reminder:** *If you are not able to sell all you produce, then you have a surplus. This would result in lower profits.*

- Explain how shortages disappear by raising prices, and how surpluses disappear by lowering prices.

4. Copy and distribute the data sheet, "Lawn Mowers," on page 25. Have students plot the supply and demand data on the graph to determine the market price and market quantity.

5. Ask students to suggest solutions for the following situations:

   - A car dealer has a surplus of current-year cars. He has just received a shipment of next year's models. How can the dealer sell current-year models quickly?
     Lower the prices on the current-year cars.

   - What will happen when a very limited number of a popular CD is produced?
     Prices will probably rise.

6. Activity

   - Divide students into four groups and provide them with the "Paper Shape Factory" worksheet on page 26.

   - The goals of each group are first, to produce with quality the assigned products, second, to end up with more money than any of the other groups, and last, to earn points for group work.

   - Supply each group with the materials listed on the worksheet. (For the money, purchase play money at a toy store or use money from the game Monopoly.) No group will have all the needed supplies. Members of each group will buy, sell, and/or trade with other groups in order to obtain the needed materials. Students will assess the marketplace (items possessed by all 4 groups) to determine which materials are in short or long supply. Groups may use only the supplies provided by the teacher.

   - Students should keep in mind that consumers will pay higher prices for materials that are in demand.

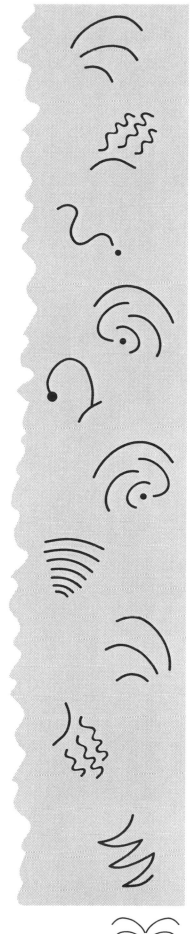

- Allow the groups 20 minutes to plan and complete the entire project. Assess their work using the stated goals as criteria.

    1. Award up to 25 points for a quality finished product.
    2. Award points equal to the number of dollars held by the group.
    3. Award up to 25 points for the written market analysis and trading plan.
    4. Award up to 25 points for positive group interaction.

    Grant awards to groups to reward their strengths (earned most money, best marketing strategy, best products, etc.).

    How well each group develops a plan, assesses the marketplace, develops strategies, and works together will be major factors influencing the quality of the products they produce. This in turn, will help determine if the group is awarded points.

7. Review the main ideas of the unit.

Demand Worksheet

Assume you have $20 to spend on compact discs (CDs). Answer each question and then plot the information on the graph below.

1. How many CDs could you buy if the price of each was four dollars? _____

2. How many CDs could you buy if the price of each was five dollars? _____

3. How many CDs could you buy if the price of each was ten dollars? _____

4. How many CDs could you buy if the price of each was twenty dollars? _____

5. What do you notice about demand as the price increases?

_____

_____

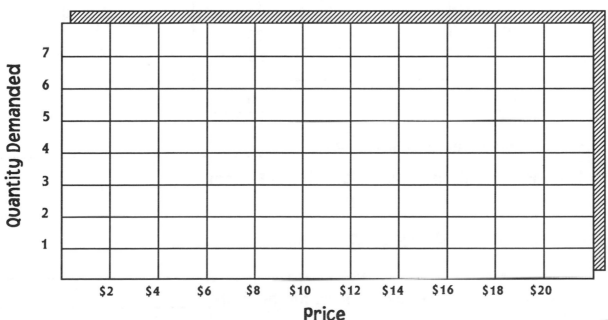

Supply Worksheet

One class of students is selling pizza slices as a fundraiser to raise money for an expensive class trip. Consider the assumptions and complete the chart. Then answer the questions.

Assumptions

- Each whole pizza costs $4.00 to make and contains 8 slices.

- There are 400 students attending the school. The class is allowed to make as many as 50 pizzas each day.

- As the price goes up, profits go up, but fewer slices will be sold.

- If the class makes too many pizzas, they must throw away leftovers.

Price Per Slice	Profit Per Pizza	Projected Number Sold	Total Profit
.40		0	
.50		50	
.60		50	
.75		40	
.80		35	
.90		30	
$1.00		20	

1. At what point does the class break even? _____

2. For what price should the class sell the pizzas? Explain. _____
   _____

3. How many pizzas should they bake? Explain. _____
   _____

4. How many days will it take to earn $600 for the trip? _____

© Instructional Fair • TS Denison   IF19311 *Social Studies Projects*

Linda's Fundraiser

Chad: "What's going on, Linda?"

Linda: "What does the sign say Chad?"

Chad: "Candy bars for sale! How much are they?"

Linda: "A dollar for one bar."

Chad: "A dollar a bar! Are you out of your mind, Linda? I can get a candy bar for 65¢ at the corner store."

Linda: But Chad, they're homemade! And I want to buy a used car. Even though my parents have agreed to pay half the cost, I still need $500.00. That's a lot of money, and I have to raise it some way."

Chad: "I don't think you will sell many candy bars at that price."

Larry: "Hey, what's going on?"

Chad: "Oh, hi, Larry, Linda has started selling homemade candy bars, but there is no way I want to pay what she's charging."

Larry: "Well, for how much are you selling them, Linda?"

Linda: "I want a dollar a bar, but Chad says that's too expensive. Chad, how much would you pay for one?"

Chad: "Because you are my friend, I might give you 75 cents for one."

Larry: "Right now, I have only 20 cents in my pocket, because I didn't get my paycheck, yet. I spent all my money when we went out this past weekend."

Linda: "Larry, there is no way I can sell a candy bar for 20 cents. I have to pay for my supplies. It cost 25 cents to make each bar.

Chad: "Here comes Mary. Let's see how much she would be willing to pay for one of your candy bars."

Mary: "Hi, everyone! Linda, it looks like you're selling candy bars."

Linda: "Yes, I am. Would you like to buy one?"

Mary: "How much are they?"

Linda: "I'm not sure. I think I'd better take a poll in class this afternoon."

Later that afternoon in class . . .

Linda: "I'm conducting a survey for a business venture I'm starting. I'd like you to answer some questions for me, and I'll record the results. Ready? Here we go.

How many of you would pay $1.00 for a candy bar? . . . None. How about 90 cents? . . . One. How about 80 cents? . . . Two. 70 cents? . . . Three. 60 cents? . . . Four. 50 cents? . . . Five. 40 cents? . . . Six.

Thank you. You've been very helpful. I'll get back to you with the results tomorrow."

Note: You will be plotting the above survey information on the graph on page 24.

Market Price and Supply

Now, plot the information from the survey Linda conducted for the demand for candy bars on the graph below.

To complete the graph below, you must also plot the number of candy bars Linda would supply at each price. Use the following information:

At $1.00, ten bars would be supplied;

at 90¢, nine bars;

at 80¢, eight bars;

at 70¢, seven bars;

at 60¢, six bars;

at 50¢, five bars;

at 40¢, four bars.

Determine at what price Linda should sell her candy bars, and how many bars must be supplied in this situation.

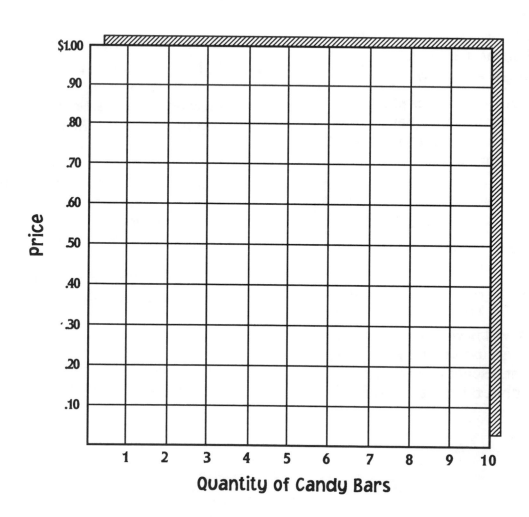

Lawn Mowers

A major lawn mower manufacturer is conducting market research so the company can determine the number of lawn mowers it should supply and at what price. Using the information gathered below, plot the supply and demand curves for lawn mowers. Then determine the market price and market supply.

Supply		Demand	
Price per lawn mower	Quantity supplied	Price per lawn mower	Quantity wanted
$700.00	12 thousand	$700.00	2 thousand
$500.00	10 thousand	$500.00	4 thousand
$400.00	8 thousand	$400.00	6 thousand
$300.00	6 thousand	$300.00	8 thousand
$200.00	4 thousand	$200.00	10 thousand
$100.00	2 thousand	$100.00	12 thousand

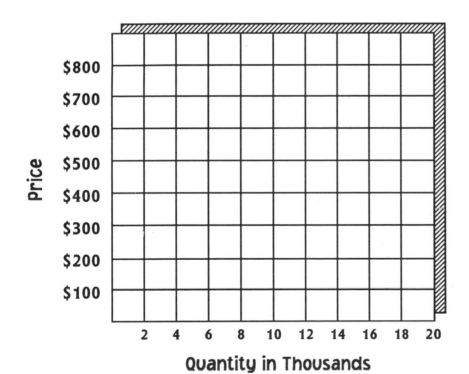

Market Price _____

Market Supply _____

Paper Shapes Factory

Problem Statement

The Paper Shapes Company produces various paper products for local businesses. Unfortunately, this week there is a shortage of all supplies needed to produce the items. However, it is your responsibility to complete the work orders to satisfy your customers. If you fail to do this, you may lose your clients and the profits that go with your work. How you solve this problem is going to require planning and strategy on the part of your team members. The future of the company depends on a satisfactory resolution. Good luck as you develop your plans and strategies!

Instructions

Each group will receive the supplies listed below. No group will have all the needed supplies. Members of each group will buy, sell, and/or trade, with other groups in order to obtain the needed materials. Your group will assess the marketplace to figure out which materials are in short or long supply. You may use only the supplies provided by your teacher; you may not use your own materials.

Group A
black, blue, red, and green paper; $25.00 in play money; and a yardstick

Group B
black and green paper; two pens; a roll of tape; $25.00 in play money; and a compass

Group C
black and blue paper; four pencils; scissors; $25.00 in play money; and one pen

Group D
blue and black paper; one pencil; a ruler; $25.00 in play money; and two pens

Each group must make the following items:

- three black triangles
- four red squares
- two intersecting blue circles with your school logo drawn with a pen inside the middle portion
- one green triangle with a frog (coin, car, or other object) drawn with a pencil

You will have 20 minutes to complete the production process.

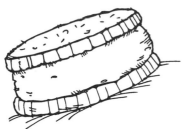

Cookie Dough Fundraiser

In addition to, or in place of the pizza slice activity suggested on pages 17, 18, and 22, you might want to conduct this fundraiser at your school as a demonstration of supply.

In this fundraising activity, students could make cookie dough to sell to family and friends. Or, students may decide to bake and then sell the cookies to students during or after school. Students will need to figure out what their supply costs are, determine how many cookies they want to bake each day, and set a price which allows for a profit, as well as is affordable for students. Students might change the price each day or week to see how cost affects sales and profits. Eventually, the students should find a price that allows for maximum profit with minimum waste. That price should then become the official price of the cookie.

This activity requires a much larger commitment than the pizza scenario presented in the lesson plan. Teachers may choose the activity which best fits their classroom needs and school situation.

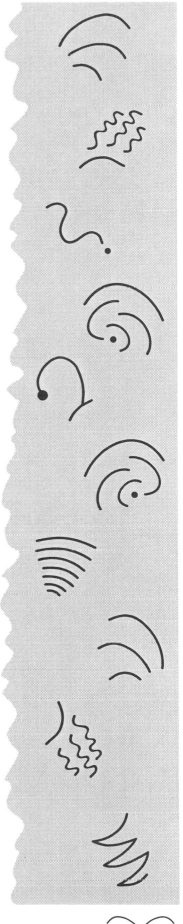

Notes

_____

_____

_____

_____

_____

_____

_____

_____

_____

_____

_____

_____

_____

_____

_____

_____

_____

_____

_____

_____

_____

_____

_____

_____

 IF19311 _Social Studies Projects_

The Stock Market

Time

One to two class periods.

Purpose

To enable students to become familiar with the stock market and how it works.

Objectives

The students will be able to . . .

- explain how the stock market works.

- pretend to buy stocks and monitor their progress for a two-week period.

Vocabulary

stock
stockholder
dividend
bull market
bear market

stock-page terminology:
high
low
close
last
net change

Concepts

- The stock market provides people with a way to invest in companies and corporations.

- People can gain or lose money in the stock market.

- People make money in the stock market by receiving dividends and selling the stock at a price higher than the purchase price.

- People lose money if they sell the stock at a price lower than the purchase price.

- The stock market is affected by many factors.

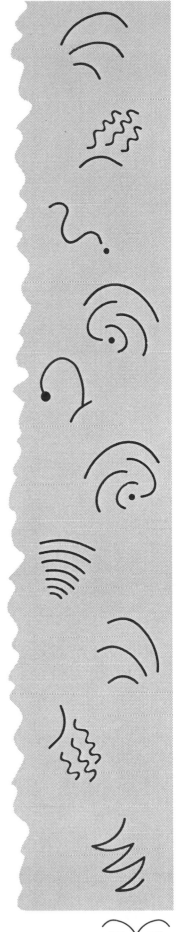

1. Discuss the purpose of the stock market.
   - Begin by asking students whether they or their parents own stock(s).
   - Explain that the stock market is *a mechanism for investing in companies.*
   - Explain that a person's goal when investing in the stock market is *to make a profit through the process of buying and selling of stocks and the receiving of dividends.*
   - Some factors that influence the stock market are *world events, weather, decisions by political leaders, wars, and so on.*

     For example, extremely cold weather could harm a crop of oranges. This could affect the stock price of any companies dealing with oranges.
   - Discuss how the factors listed above, plus any generated by the students, could affect the stock market.

2. Present the following terms:

   Stock—*share of ownership in a business.*

   Stockholder—*person who owns a share of stock.*

   Dividend—*a share of the profits.*
   The more stock one owns, the greater one's share of the dividends.

   Bull Market—*period of time when stock prices consistently rise.*

   Bear Market—*period of time when stock prices consistently fall.*

3. Distribute copies of the stock pages from the newspaper or use computers to show a stock page on the screen. One location found on the Internet is **InvestSmart**. You can locate it at: **library.advanced.org/10326/**
   - Discuss the meanings of the following entries from the stock report:

     Name—*This is the name of the company or corporation, usually in the form of an abbreviation.*

High—*highest price at which the stock sold during the last trading session.*

Low—*lowest price at which the stock sold during the last trading session.*

Close or Last—*price of the stock at the end of the last trading session.*

Net Change—*how much each share of stock went up or down from the day's opening of the market to the day's close of the market.*

- Point out that the quotes in the newspapers are usually from the previous day's activity.

- Use several examples for discussion and explanation.

- Have students pick any stock from the paper or computer, and have them follow the progress of the stock for one to two weeks.

  - Students will buy 100 shares of the stock, using the closing price. (If you have access to up-to-the-minute quotes, feel free to use those instead of the closing prices.)

  - Each day, students will write the closing price on their "Stock Chart" on page 35.

  - At the end of the period, students will sell their stock, using the closing price. (Again, if you have access to up-to-the-minute quotes, feel free to use those instead of the closing prices.)

    The teacher might want to charge students a stockbroker fee before calculating total profit or loss. If not, be sure to discuss stockbrokers and fees.

- Review how each student did in the market. Remind students that they probably would remain in the market for a much longer period of time in real life.

4. Activity

- Divide students into small groups. Each group will choose a spokesperson.

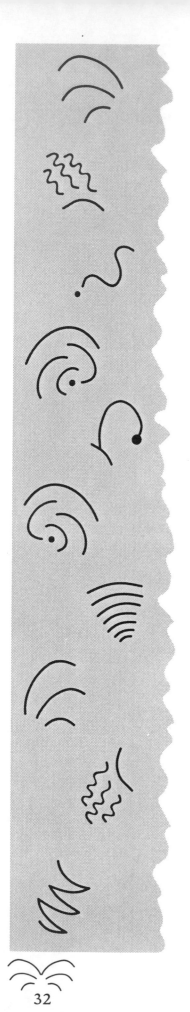

- Give each group an imaginary $1,000 to buy stock in a professional sports team. (You will need to determine which professional sports league to follow.)

- Currently, stock is selling for $20.00 a share. Students will make their own stock purchases in blocks of five. They can buy 5, 10, 15 shares, and so on.

- Students must decide whether to invest all of their money in stocks or to keep some to put into a savings account for the purpose of buying future stocks.

   Remind students that their goal is to make as much money as they can as they go through the seven events of this activity.

   Use the "Stock Market Activity Chart" on page 36 to keep track of each group's totals. (You may prefer to do this on the board as the figures will change from round to round. Students will also keep track in their groups.)

   Begin filling in the charts as each group announces its purchase.

- Inform students that from this point on, various events will take place that will influence the sports club and will have an effect on the price of the stock. Students will try to analyze how the stock price will be affected and then make appropriate decisions (buying, selling, or keeping what they have) in order to maximize the value of their group's stock. If they buy or sell, it must always be in blocks of five.

   As you announce each event, students in each group will make a joint decision regarding their stock (buy, sell, or hold). After each group has made its decision, the teacher will announce the new stock price, and new group values will be calculated.

IF19311 *Social Studies Projects*

- **Events**
    1. **The sports team wins its division and will continue to play in the elimination series for the championship.**
        a. Students now decide whether to buy, sell, or take no action.
        b. Announce the new stock price of $40.00 per share.
        c. Students calculate the new value of each group's stock.

    2. **The club's star players begin to experience a decline in their level of play.**
        a. Students will decide to buy, sell, or take no action.
        b. Announce the new stock price of $15.00 per share.
        c. Calculate the new value of each group's stock.

    3. **The state announces plans to build a prison directly across the street from the stadium where the team plays.**
        a. Students will decide to buy, sell, or take no action.
        b. Announce the new stock price of $5.00 per share.
        c. Calculate the new value of each group's stock.

    4. **The club signs some young, talented players who should help the club tremendously in the future.**
        a. Students will decide to buy, sell, or take no action.
        b. Announce the new stock price of $15.00 per share.
        c. Calculate the new value of each group's stock.

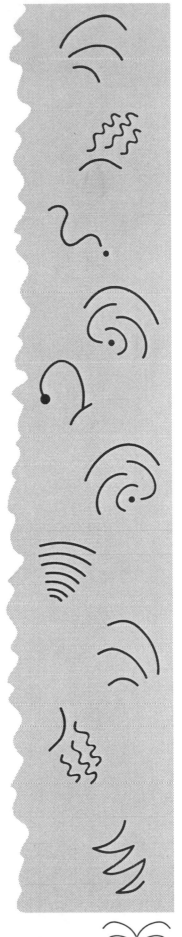

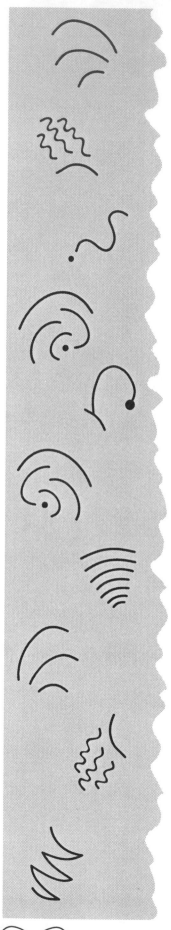

5. **The players go on strike.**
   a. Students will decide to buy, sell, or take no action.
   b. Announce the new stock price of $8.00 per share.
   c. Calculate the new value of each group's stock.

6. **The sports league signs a lucrative television contract and develops a revenue-sharing plan.** (You may have to explain these concepts to the students.)
   a. Students will decide to buy, sell, or take no action.
   b. Announce the new stock price of $25.00 per share.
   c. Calculate the new value of each group's stock.

7. **The team announces plans to build a new stadium.**
   a. Students will decide to buy, sell, or take no action.
   b. Announce the new stock price of $35.00 per share.
   c. Calculate the new value of each group's stock.

- Compare records to see which group made the most money.

   Have each group's spokesperson explain the strategies the group used. *They should focus on purchasing at low prices and selling at high prices, although other strategies may be acceptable.*

5. Review the main ideas of the lesson.

© Instructional Fair • TS Denison   IF19311 *Social Studies Projects*

Stock Chart

Choose a stock to follow for the next two weeks. Fill in the information about your stock in the box below. Then track the information that you find in the newspaper on the chart.

Date of purchase _____

Name of your stock _____

Price per share _____

Number of shares you wish to buy _____

Total cost _____

Date	High	Low	Close	Net Change

At the end of the two-week period, complete the following analysis.

1. High price per share during the past two weeks: _____

2. At that price, what would have been the total value of your stock? _____

3. Lowest price per share during the past two weeks: _____

4. At that price, what would have been the total value of your stock? _____

5. Price of your stock at the end of the two-week period: _____

6. Net profit or loss per share: _____

7. Total profit or loss (Multiply last figure by number of shares.): _____

Stock Market Activity Chart

Complete the chart.

Event	Trans-action	Number of Shares Bought or Sold	Price Per Share	Transaction Amount	Total Shares Owned	Value of Shares Owned	Cash in the Bank	Total Assets
Beginning Balance	None	0	$20	$0	0	$0	$1,000	$1,000
Initial Investment	Buy							
1								
2								
3								
4								
5								
6								
7								

Notes

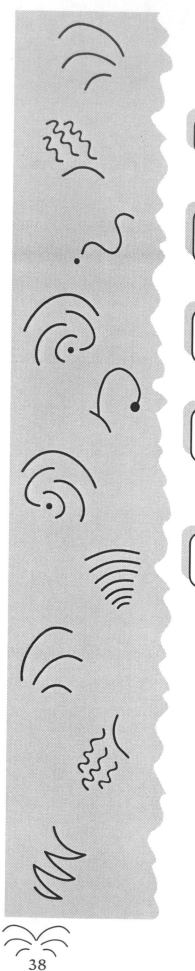

Capitalism, Communism, and Socialism

Time

Two class periods.

Purpose

To enable students to understand that other economies are different from ours.

Objective

Students will identify the three main economic systems operating in the world, and explain how they differ from one another.

Vocabulary

capitalism	capital
communism	finished products
socialism	strike
labor	free choice
means of production	

Concepts

- In a capitalist society, private citizens own most of the businesses and industries and therefore maintain most of the control and decision-making power.

- In a communist society, the government maintains control and ownership of virtually all business and industry.

- In a socialist society, there is a fairly equal combination of government control and private ownership. With socialism, the government usually controls very large industries such as railroads, electricity, and gas. Private individuals usually control smaller businesses.

- In economies with more severe restrictions, there is usually less activity in the economy.

© Instructional Fair • TS Denison   IF19311 *Social Studies Projects*

1. Define the following terms:

   a. Means of Production—*includes land, labor and capital. Labor is the work force. Capital is the money and resources used for investment in a project.*

   b. Finished Products—*goods manufactured in an economy.*

   c. Strike—*Workers refuse to work, often because there is no contractual agreement reached after the old contract expires.*

   d. Free Choice—*People are able to make their own decisions without outside interference.*

2. Place the following on the board and discuss.

Economic System	Means of Production & Finished Goods	Freedom of Choice	Role of Government in Economy	Examples
Capitalism	Privately owned & controlled	Much	Limited government involvement	U.S. Canada
Socialism	Privately & government controlled	Much/ Varies	Some government involvement	France Germany
Communism	Government controlled	Very little, if any	Much government involvement	China Cuba

3. Place the following continuum on the board.

| Communism | Socialism | Capitalism |

   a. Point out that no country's economy is totally capitalist or totally communist.

   b. For example, China has some privately owned businesses, and the U.S. has government regulations on what businesses can and cannot do (i.e., child labor laws).

   c. Indicate where some countries would be located along the continuum.

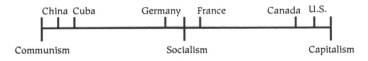

China Cuba   Germany France   Canada U.S.

Communism   Socialism   Capitalism

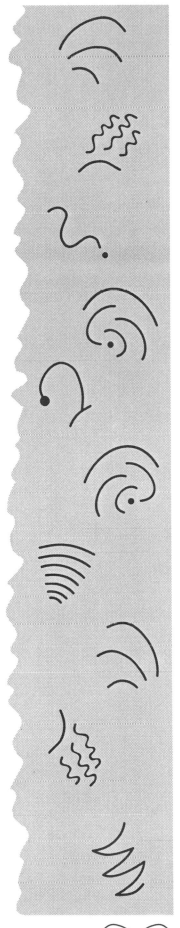

4. Activity
   - Provide the following supplies:

     twenty-five cents per student (one dime, two nickels, and five pennies)

     candy

     looseleaf paper

     pencils

     small Post-it Notes
   - Divide the class into three groups. Each group will represent one of the economic systems: communist; socialist; or capitalist.
   - First, role-play the communist economy.
     - Choose a total of four students from the socialist and/or capitalist economic groups to act as sellers. Set up four shopping areas in the classroom with each person selling one of the four products listed above.
     - Have the students representing the communist system line up to get their money. *You should be slow and inefficient when performing this task which is typical in communist economic systems.*
     - Tell the students they will be able to use the money to buy products from the four students who are selling.
     - Inform the sellers that providing good, courteous service is not important since they cannot set their own prices nor control the amount of profit they make.
     - Write on the board how much each product is worth. (There will be no exceptions or modifications of these prices during the activity.)
       a. one piece of candy—2¢
       b. one sheet of looseleaf paper—3¢
       c. one pencil—6¢
       d. one notepad—12¢
       e. one pencil—three pieces of candy
       f. two sheets of looseleaf paper—three pieces of candy

     g. one notepad—six pieces of candy

     h. one pencil—two sheets of looseleaf paper

     i. one notepad—two pencils

     j. one notepad—four sheets of looseleaf paper

- Allow students three or four minutes to shop.

- Discuss the the characteristics of the system just illustrated. Ask students to describe their feelings regarding waiting in line for the money, the establishment of prices by the government, and the service and attitude of the sellers.

- Next, role-play the socialist economy.

  - Tell students equality is very important in this economic system. Focus on how the government has stressed that everyone and everything should be equal for all citizens.

  - Choose four students from the communist and/or capitalist groups to act as sellers. Set up as in the first example.

  - Pass out the money to the students in the socialist group. *You will be as efficient as possible in distributing the money.*

  - Tell the students they will be able to use the money to buy products from the four students who are selling.

  - Inform the sellers that providing good, courteous service is important since they can set their own prices, and therefore influence the profit they may make.

  - Sellers will set their own prices.

  - Allow students three or four minutes to shop.

  - When time is up, check to see if each buyer has an equal value of products. If not, have students redistribute products among themselves so everyone has approximately the same amount of each product or products of equivalent value.

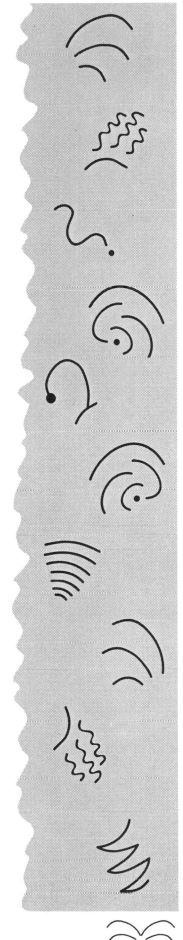

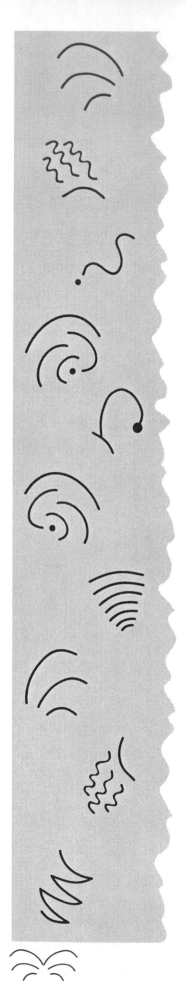

- Discuss the characteristics of this system. Ask students to describe how they felt about the government's actions at the end of the activity. Also, ask students how they felt about the ability to have prices set by the sellers instead of the government. Check student responses as to the quality of service provided.
- Finally, role-play the capitalist economy.
  - Set up as in the first two examples, except this time it is the capitalists who are the buyers.
  - If you want to take the extra time, pass out varying amounts of the money to the students in the capitalist group. (In capitalist societies, there is more often greater disparity of incomes.) *You will be as efficient as possible in distributing the money.*
  - Tell the students they will be able to use the money to buy products from the four students who are selling.
  - Inform the sellers that providing good, courteous service is important since they can set their own prices, and therefore influence the profit they may make.
  - Allow students three or four minutes to shop.
  - Discuss the characteristics of this system. Ask students to describe how they felt about income differences, the freedom they had, and the ability to have prices set by the sellers instead of by the government. Check student responses as to the quality of service provided by the sellers.
- Discuss with the class the positive and negative aspects of each system.
5. Point out that our system is a capitalist one. Point out that there are examples of government control in our system.
   - Discuss some of the laws and regulations of government control.
   - Mention that the laws are intended to prevent abuses by people or corporations, such as the formation of monopolies.
6. Review the main ideas of the unit.

© Instructional Fair • TS Denison   IF19311 *Social Studies Projects*

Notes

_____

_____

_____

_____

_____

_____

_____

_____

_____

_____

_____

_____

_____

_____

_____

_____

_____

_____

_____

_____

_____

_____

_____

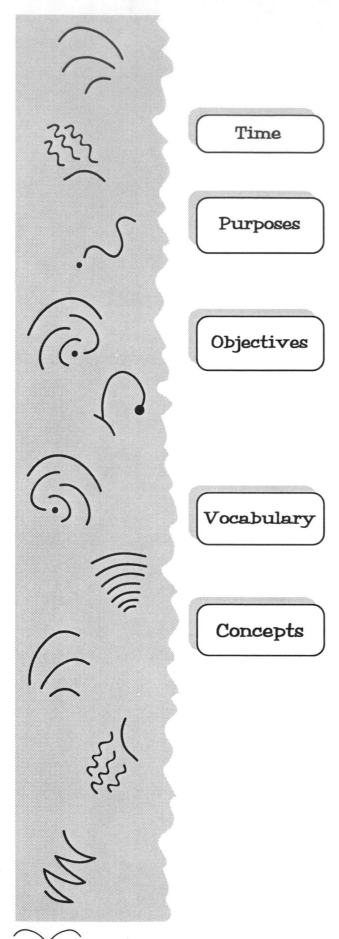

Money and Banking

Time

Two to three class periods.

Purposes

- To enable students to understand the role money plays in our society.
- To enable students to learn how to write a check and balance a checkbook.

Objectives

The students will be able to . . .

- explain why money is used in our economy.
- explain the purpose of banks and describe some of their services.
- write a check and balance a checkbook.

Vocabulary

money	interest	transaction
barter	checks	credit
banks	deposit	income
loans	withdrawal	expenses

Concepts

- Money is used in our economy to make our lives more efficient.
- Before money, people bartered for items they needed or wanted.
- Banks are in business to make a profit.
- Banks provide many services.
- Many factors are involved in determining whether a person is approved for a loan by the bank.
- Writing a check and balancing a checkbook is an important life skill.

 IF19311 *Social Studies Projects*

<table>
<tr><td>

Procedures & Teaching Ideas

</td></tr>
</table>

1. Have students consider the role money plays in their lives.

   Students should consider the necessity, the uses, and the availability of money.

2. Provide a definition for *money*.

   Money is an accepted medium of exchange for products and services.

3. Ask students to imagine a community where money as we know it does not exist. Discuss the following concepts.

   • Provide a definition for *barter—**an economic activity whereby people trade goods for the items they need.***

   • Pretend a person makes shoes for a living. However, this person also needs food and clothing. How would he/she go about getting these items?

   • What would happen if the meat and clothing producers didn't need shoes? How could the shoemaker get those items if he/she couldn't make the exchange? (Find a third person to enter the trade.)

   • How much food is equal to the value of a pair of shoes?

   • What advantages are there to bartering? *Very few.* What disadvantages are there to bartering? *People have to search to find someone willing to trade. If they can't, they may be unable to get the goods and services they want or need.*

   • Discuss how using money makes trading more efficient. *Money would be the exchange for the needed goods or services.*

4. Ask students what they do with any surplus money they don't plan to spend right away.

   Some students will respond that they put it in a bank.

5. Shift the lesson to a discussion about banks and their services. Write the word *banks* on the

board. Ask students to explain why most people put money in a bank instead of keeping it at home.

Students should mention the safety a bank provides as well as the payment of interest.

- Write the term *interest* on the board.

    Define *interest* as *payment for borrowing money from another.*

    Explain how interest works. Assume a deposit of $1,000 is made for one year at 4% annual interest. At the end of one year, the account would have $1,040. The $40.00 is the payment by the bank for allowing it to use your money.

6. Discuss some services banks provide for their customers.

    - Loans

        People go to the bank to borrow money for various purposes. These include buying houses and cars, paying tuition, and paying off large bills.

        Pass out the sample "Loan Application Form" on page 48 and discuss its parts.

        Focus discussion on the monthly income a person has in comparison to the monthly expenses. Having greater expenses with a smaller income may reduce the chances of getting a loan.

        Discuss prior credit history. A good credit history increases the likelihood of receiving a loan.

    - Savings Accounts

        People put money into a bank savings account to earn interest.

    - Checking Accounts

        Checks are a written order to your bank to pay someone a specific amount of money out of your checking account.

7. Discuss how banks make a profit.

    - Banks will pay interest to people who deposit

money in certain accounts. Banks take the money that people deposit in savings and checking accounts and loan it to other people. The bank charges them a higher interest rate than the bank pays you for your deposit. Banks also invest your money in stocks and other investments that pay a higher rate of interest than the bank pays you.

- Banks charge fees for special services. These include money orders, electronic transfers, and stopping payment on a check.

- Stress that banks are in business to make money. All the nice things they do are designed to attract customers which should enhance a bank's ability to make money.

8. Present the check-writing activity and assignment.

- Copy and distribute the sample deposit slips on page 49 and explain how to use them.

- Copy and distribute the check samples on page 50 and explain how to fill one out. Point out the different check components and provide students with names and amounts to fill in.

- Show students how to keep a record of deposits and withdrawals by distributing and discussing the information on the "Recording Checks" handout on page 51.

- Distribute copies of the "Check-Writing Assignment" on page 52. Hand out clean copies of checks, deposit slips, and the "Check Register" sheet (pages 53–56) to each student.

- Have students complete the assignment independently. You may want to do the first step or two with less able students to get them started.

9. Review the main ideas of the unit.

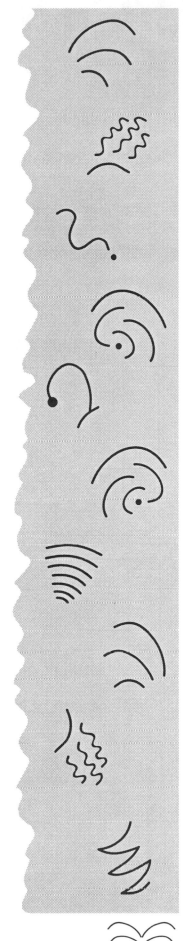

Loan Application Form

Name _____ Age _____

Street address _____

City _____

State, Zip code _____ _____

Home phone number _____

Length of time at current address _____

Current Occupation _____

      Monthly income $ _____

      Monthly expenses $_____

      Net monthly income $ _____

List two references (not relatives) and their phone numbers.

  1. _____ _____

  2. _____ _____

Purpose of Loan _____

Amount of loan desired $ _____

Length of loan in months _____

For Bank Use Only

Approved: ☐ Yes   ☐ No

Interest rate _____ %   Monthly payments $ _____

Length of loan in months _____

© Instructional Fair • TS Denison   IF19311 *Social Studies Projects*

ACCOUNT NO. 00–00–0000	CASH	CURRENCY		
		COIN		
DATE_____		LIST CHECKS SINGLY		
NAME _____				
☐ CHECKING DEPOSIT		TOTAL		
		LESS CASH RECEIVED		
☐ SAVINGS DEPOSIT		NET DEPOSIT		

DEPOSIT

DEPOSITS MAY NOT BE AVAILABLE FOR IMMEDIATE WITHDRAWAL

$ *DOLLAR STATE BANK* $

ACCOUNT NO. 00–00–0000	CASH	CURRENCY		
		COIN		
DATE_____		LIST CHECKS SINGLY		
NAME _____				
☐ CHECKING DEPOSIT		TOTAL		
		LESS CASH RECEIVED		
☐ SAVINGS DEPOSIT		NET DEPOSIT		

DEPOSIT

DEPOSITS MAY NOT BE AVAILABLE FOR IMMEDIATE WITHDRAWAL

$ *DOLLAR STATE BANK* $

ACCOUNT NO. 00–00–0000	CASH	CURRENCY		
		COIN		
DATE_____		LIST CHECKS SINGLY		
NAME _____				
☐ CHECKING DEPOSIT		TOTAL		
		LESS CASH RECEIVED		
☐ SAVINGS DEPOSIT		NET DEPOSIT		

DEPOSIT

DEPOSITS MAY NOT BE AVAILABLE FOR IMMEDIATE WITHDRAWAL

$ *DOLLAR STATE BANK* $

ACCOUNT NO. 00–00–0000	CASH	CURRENCY		
		COIN		
DATE_____		LIST CHECKS SINGLY		
NAME _____				
☐ CHECKING DEPOSIT		TOTAL		
		LESS CASH RECEIVED		
☐ SAVINGS DEPOSIT		NET DEPOSIT		

DEPOSIT

DEPOSITS MAY NOT BE AVAILABLE FOR IMMEDIATE WITHDRAWAL

$ *DOLLAR STATE BANK* $

Sam Cash
7777 Money Way
Milwaukee, WI 53001

0000
73-00003872

November 23, 19 *99*

PAY TO THE
ORDER OF   *John Kree* $ *35.00*

Thirty five and 00/100 ——————— Dollars

🔒 Security Features
Included
Details on back

$ **DOLLAR STATE BANK** $

For *Stereo system parts*   *Sam Cash*   MP

⑆180009999⑆⑈10000000300⑉

0000
73-00003872

19

PAY TO THE
ORDER OF $

Dollars 🔒 Security Features
Included
Details on back

$ **DOLLAR STATE BANK** $

For   MP

⑆180009999⑆⑈10000000300⑉

0000
73-00003872

19

PAY TO THE
ORDER OF $

Dollars 🔒 Security Features
Included
Details on back

$ **DOLLAR STATE BANK** $

For   MP

⑆180009999⑆⑈10000000300⑉

Recording Checks

1. Check #2376, written to John Kree for $35.00 on May 10.

2. Check #2377, written to Bud Rose for $20.05 on May 14.

3. Deposited $50.00 to my account on May 22.

4. Check #2378, written to J.S. for $318.23 on May 22.

Number	Date	Description of Transaction	Payment/ Debit (−)		✔ T	Fee (If any) (−)	Deposit/ Credit (+)	Balance
								$ 575.00
2376	5/10	John Kree	35	00				−35.00
								540.00
2377	5/14	Bud Rose	20	05				−20.05
								519.95
	5/22	Deposit					50.00	+50.00
								569.95
2378	5/22	J.S.	318	23				−318.23
								251.72

Check-Writing Assignment

1. Start the month by opening your account with a $500.00 deposit on February 1. Use a deposit slip.

2. Write check #234 on February 7th to Fairbank's Bakery for $12.00. (Bought bread, a pie, and a cake.)

3. Write check number #235 on February 11 to Evan's Shoe Store for $70.41. (Bought tennis shoes.)

4. Make a deposit of $120.50 on February 14. Use a deposit slip.

5. Write check #236 on February 22 to Charities, Inc. for $10.00. (Charitable contribution)

6. Write check #237 to Sam's Travel Service for $350.00 on February 25. (Plane ticket)

7. Write check #238 to Bill's Barber Shop for $13.50 on February 28. (Haircut and styling)

8. Make a deposit of $150.00 on February 28. Use a deposit slip.

Check 1

0000

73-00003872

19 _____

PAY TO THE
ORDER OF _____

$ [   ]

Dollars 🔒 Security Features
Included
Details on back

$ **DOLLAR STATE BANK** $

For _____

MP

⑈1⁞80009999⑈1⑈0000000300 ⌐⌐⌐⌐

Check 2

0000

73-00003872

19 _____

PAY TO THE
ORDER OF _____

$ [   ]

Dollars 🔒 Security Features
Included
Details on back

$ **DOLLAR STATE BANK** $

For _____

MP

⑈1⁞80009999⑈1⑈0000000300 ⌐⌐⌐⌐

Check 3

0000

73-00003872

19 _____

PAY TO THE
ORDER OF _____

$ [   ]

Dollars 🔒 Security Features
Included
Details on back

$ **DOLLAR STATE BANK** $

For _____

MP

⑈1⁞80009999⑈1⑈0000000300 ⌐⌐⌐⌐

Check 1

0000

73-00003872

19 _____

PAY TO THE
ORDER OF _____ $ [   ]

Dollars | 🔒 Security Features Included / Details on back

$ **DOLLAR STATE BANK** $

For _____ _____ MP

⑊ 1800099991 ⑊ 10000000300 ⑊⑊

Check 2

0000

73-00003872

19 _____

PAY TO THE
ORDER OF _____ $ [   ]

Dollars | 🔒 Security Features Included / Details on back

$ **DOLLAR STATE BANK** $

For _____ _____ MP

⑊ 1800099991 ⑊ 10000000300 ⑊⑊

Check 3

0000

73-00003872

19 _____

PAY TO THE
ORDER OF _____ $ [   ]

Dollars | 🔒 Security Features Included / Details on back

$ **DOLLAR STATE BANK** $

For _____ _____ MP

⑊ 1800099991 ⑊ 10000000300 ⑊⑊

© Instructional Fair • TS Denison   IF19311 *Social Studies Projects*

ACCOUNT NO. 00–00–0000	CASH	CURRENCY			DEPOSIT
		COIN			
DATE_____		LIST CHECKS SINGLY			
NAME _____					
☐ CHECKING DEPOSIT		TOTAL			
		LESS CASH RECEIVED			
☐ SAVINGS DEPOSIT		NET DEPOSIT			

DEPOSITS MAY NOT BE AVAILABLE FOR IMMEDIATE WITHDRAWAL $ *DOLLAR STATE BANK* $

— — — — — — — — — — — — — — — — —

ACCOUNT NO. 00–00–0000	CASH	CURRENCY			DEPOSIT
		COIN			
DATE_____		LIST CHECKS SINGLY			
NAME _____					
☐ CHECKING DEPOSIT		TOTAL			
		LESS CASH RECEIVED			
☐ SAVINGS DEPOSIT		NET DEPOSIT			

DEPOSITS MAY NOT BE AVAILABLE FOR IMMEDIATE WITHDRAWAL $ *DOLLAR STATE BANK* $

— —

ACCOUNT NO. 00–00–0000	CASH	CURRENCY			DEPOSIT
		COIN			
DATE_____		LIST CHECKS SINGLY			
NAME _____					
☐ CHECKING DEPOSIT		TOTAL			
		LESS CASH RECEIVED			
☐ SAVINGS DEPOSIT		NET DEPOSIT			

DEPOSITS MAY NOT BE AVAILABLE FOR IMMEDIATE WITHDRAWAL $ *DOLLAR STATE BANK* $

— —

ACCOUNT NO. 00–00–0000	CASH	CURRENCY			DEPOSIT
		COIN			
DATE_____		LIST CHECKS SINGLY			
NAME _____					
☐ CHECKING DEPOSIT		TOTAL			
		LESS CASH RECEIVED			
☐ SAVINGS DEPOSIT		NET DEPOSIT			

DEPOSITS MAY NOT BE AVAILABLE FOR IMMEDIATE WITHDRAWAL $ *DOLLAR STATE BANK* $

— —

Check Register

Number	Date	Description of Transaction	Payment/ Debit (−)		Fee (If any) (−)	Deposit/ Credit (+)		Balance	

© Instructional Fair • TS Denison   IF19311 *Social Studies Projects*

Notes

_____

_____

_____

_____

_____

_____

_____

_____

_____

_____

_____

_____

_____

_____

_____

_____

_____

_____

_____

_____

_____

_____

_____

_____

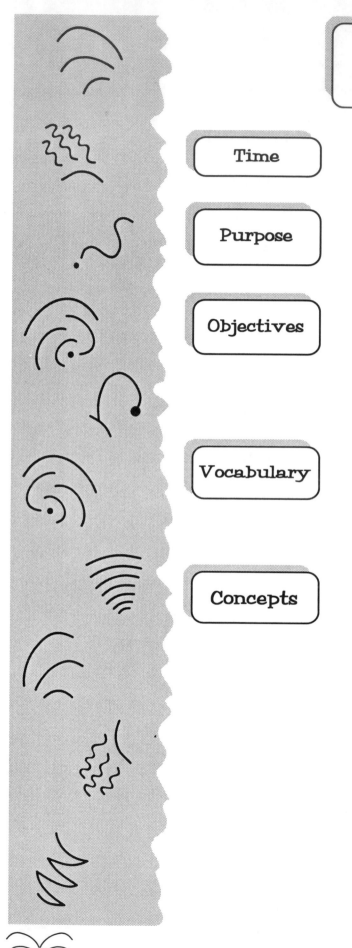

Unions and Collective Bargaining

Time

One to two class periods.

Purpose

To enable students to understand the purposes of unions and the concept of collective bargaining.

Objectives

Students will be able to . . .

• explain the purposes of unions.

• identify the activities of unions.

• demonstrate how the process of collective bargaining works.

Vocabulary

unions	strike
picketing	contract
slowdown	collective bargaining
boycott	management

Concepts

• Immigration and industrialization changed the workplace in many ways. For workers, it led to dramatically different working conditions, usually very unpleasant. As a result, labor unions formed to help workers.

• Union workers may employ a variety of tactics to pressure management to bring about a contract settlement.

• Collective bargaining is the negotiation process organized workers and management use to reach a new contract. It may be a short or a lengthy process, depending on several factors.

• Contracts have many components, all of which have an impact on both management and the workforce.

© Instructional Fair • TS Denison   IF19311 *Social Studies Projects*

<table>
<tr><td>

Procedures & Teaching Ideas
</td><td>

1. Begin by asking whether any students have family members who belong to a union.

   - Ask if anyone understands what unions are and what their purpose is.

   - A union can be defined as *a group of laborers organized to secure good wages and working conditions; to protect workers' rights; and to safeguard workers' jobs.* (Feel free to give examples of each of the components of the definition.)

   - The goals of unions include receiving good wages; having reasonable working hours; maintaining and improving the working environment; and saving and protecting jobs.

2. Review with students why unions formed.

   - With more and more immigrants arriving in the U.S., there was an oversupply of workers.

   - As more people began working in factories and the size of the factories increased, wages decreased and working conditions deteriorated.

   - In order to improve their lot, the workers banded together to act as a group, rather than individually. This way more pressure could be brought upon the employer to make changes.

3. Explain that the term *contract* refers to *a legal document that covers all conditions of employment between the union (workers) and the company.*

4. Engage students in a discussion regarding the ways unions can bring pressure upon the employer or company to revise a contract. (Listed below from least to most severe are employee actions you may introduce to students.)

   - *Informational picketing*—Workers march with signs outside the place of employment. This is usually done peacefully.
</td></tr>
</table>

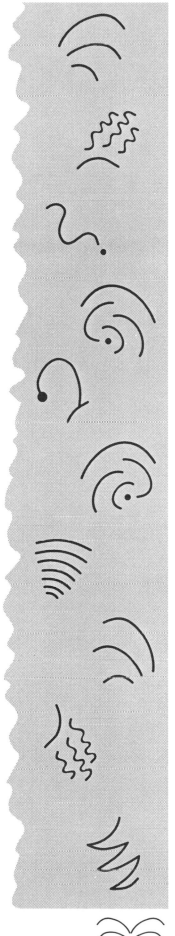

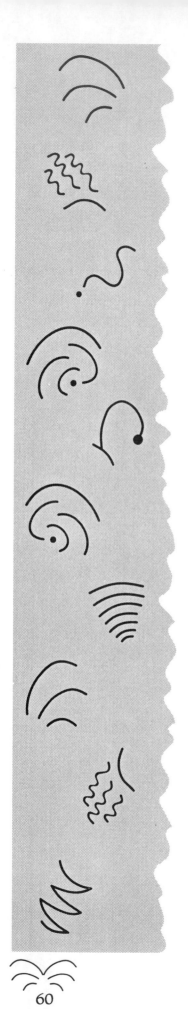

- *Withdrawal of special services*—Workers do nothing beyond their basic jobs. Participation in company-sponsored extracurricular activities stops. These may include community fundraisers, picnics, or recreational activities.

- *Slowdown*—Workers go to work but work at a slower pace than normal.

- *Boycott*—The union urges its members and the community not to purchase the products produced.

- *Strike*—Workers refuse to work. A strike is often a very difficult situation for both workers and employers. Workers don't get paid during a strike and, quite possibly, they may lose their jobs. They may also not recover lost wages. It becomes a major hardship if the strike is long.

5. Introduce the concept of *Collective Bargaining*. This refers to **the practice of the union and the company sitting down face to face to try to reach a new contractual agreement.**

   - Collective bargaining may last several months or longer, or it could be a relatively short process. *For example, the major league baseball negotiations took years to settle.*

   - Point out that occasionally the government helps settle a strike. *In 1993, the government pushed American Airlines' flight attendants to settle a strike so that their walkout would not cripple thousands of Thankgiving holiday travelers.*

   - When an old contract expires, both sides may agree to extend it until a new agreement is reached.

6. Activity.

   - Distribute copies of "Current Contract for Excel School Supplies Corporation" on page 62. Be sure to explain each element. For example, discuss the concept of a percentage pay increase for all workers versus a flat rate (25¢ an hour) increase for all workers. Also, discuss the concept of insurance, sick days, and other provisions which students may not understand.

- Distribute copies of the "Problem Statement" on page 63 and discuss.

- Divide students into groups of four. In each group, two students will represent management, while the other two students will represent the labor union.

- Before starting to negotiate, the two management representatives and the two union representatives will meet only with their partners to discuss possible changes in the contract. The goal of management is to produce a quality product and earn the highest profit possible. The goal of the union is to have reasonable working conditions and the highest pay possible. When both sides are ready, they will come face to face in negotiations (collective bargaining). Allow twenty to twenty-five minutes. (Groups that can't reach an agreement may need to meet during the lunch break or before/after school to finish the negotiations. This will help students realize how negotiations which don't go smoothly cause inconvenience in the lives of the negotiators.)

- Students will write down the terms of the new agreement as they negotiate the proposed "Union Personnel Contract for Excel School Supply Corporation" worksheet on page 64. Students should be very specific and detailed when completing the information. The final contract must be signed by both management and labor representatives. When all groups have finished . . .

    - students will share their thoughts about the process and what their group did or did not accomplish.

    - students will discuss what factors allowed the groups to operate smoothly or to experience difficulties. Feel free to offer your opinion of the new contract developed by each group. Discuss the strengths and weaknesses of the negotiated documents.

7. Review the main concepts of the lesson.

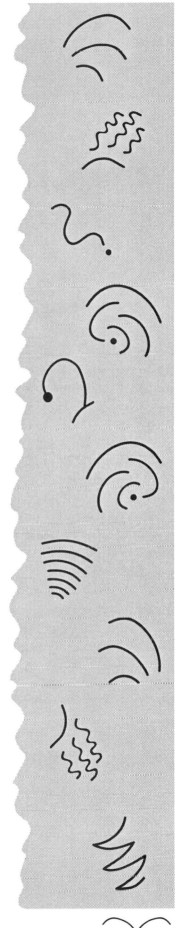

Current Contract for
Excel School Supply Corporation

Pay Scale:

$5.50 to $7.75 an hour depending on length of service.

0–1 year $5.50	6–8 years $7.00
1–3 years $6.00	9–12 years $7.40
4–5 years $6.50	Over 13 years $7.75

Overtime Provisions:

Time and a half for working any hours over 40 hours a week. Double-time for Sundays and holidays.

Paid Holidays:

New Year's Day, Memorial Day, July 4, Labor Day, Thanksgiving Day and the following Friday, Christmas Eve and Christmas Day, New Year's Day

Note:

All workers will be given three personal days with pay.
(This will allow for celebration of other religious holidays.)

Vacation:

Zero to six weeks depending on length of service.

0–1 year—no vacation	10–12 years—4 weeks
1–3 years—1 week	13–17 years—5 weeks
4–6 years—2 weeks	Over 18 years—6 weeks
7–9 years—3 weeks	

Sick Days:

Ten days per year. Unused sick days may be accumulated up to 150 days.

Insurance:

The company pays for health, dental, and vision insurance.

Length of Current Contract:

2 years

© Instructional Fair • TS Denison   IF19311 *Social Studies Projects*

Problem Statement

The Excel School Supply Corporation in Middleville, Wisconsin, produces supplies for schools. This company has about 55 employees, most of whom work full-time. The workers are represented by a union that has a good working relationship with company management. There have been no strikes during the company's history. The union and the company have always agreed to and signed contracts lasting two years.

The present contract expires at noon tomorrow. The union and management have been negotiating a new contract for the past two months. In the last few years, the company has made a profit of 10.8%. However, the inflation rate during the same period was 5.4%, and it seems to be creeping steadily upward. The company is also very concerned about the increasing cost of health insurance which is rising at about 10% a year. The company currently pays about $7,500 per year for each worker who has a family health insurance plan, and about $3,750 per year for each worker who has an individual health insurance plan.

The management wants to continue its good relationship with the union. However, the main objective of management is to maximize profits for the company and its shareholders. Rising health insurance costs threaten to cut into the company's profits.

The union negotiators must consider what would happen if the rate of inflation changes. A rise in the inflation rate during the duration of the new contract could mean the workers would earn less money in real dollar terms.

> Time is running out for a settlement before the present contract expires. Familiarize yourself with the issues and begin the final negotiation process within your groups.

Union Personnel Contract for
Excel School Supply Corporation

Pay Scale: _____   _____

_____   _____

_____   _____

_____   _____

Hours per week: _____

Overtime Provisions: _____

Hours of the Workday: _____

Paid Holidays:

_____

_____

Personal Days: _____

Vacation: _____   _____

_____   _____

_____   _____

_____   _____

Sick Days: _____

Insurance: _____

_____

Length of Current Contract (in years): _____

The management and union of the Excel School Supply Corporation agree to the above written terms of this contract.

Management Signatures

_____   _____

Union Signatures

_____   _____

Date: _____

IF19311 *Social Studies Projects*

Notes

_____

_____

_____

_____

_____

_____

_____

_____

_____

_____

_____

_____

_____

_____

_____

_____

_____

_____

_____

_____

_____

_____

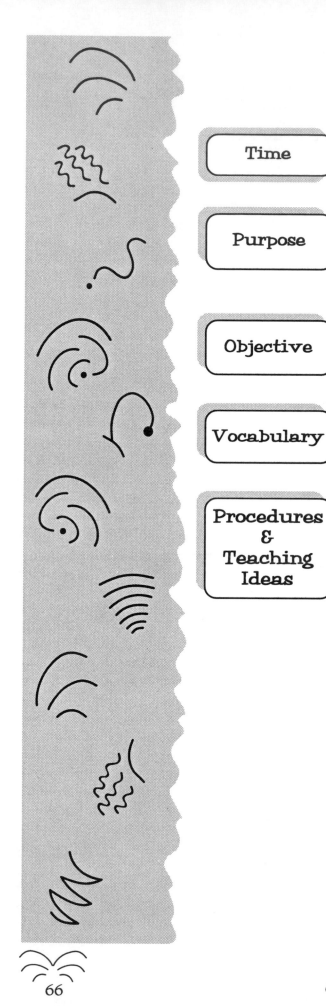

Time

One class period.

Purpose

To enable students to become proficient at reading map directions.

Objective

Students will be able to interpret directions on a map.

Vocabulary

compass rose

Procedures & Teaching Ideas

1. Have students define *compass rose*.

2. Remind students that . . .

   - all maps have at least an arrow indicating *north*. North is usually at the top of a map. The following diagram is an example of a compass rose. This one indicates all directions.

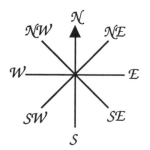

   - the sun always rises in the east and sets in the west.

3. Make copies of and hand out the "Mapping Activity" on pages 67 and 68.

Mapping Activity

Use the map of Wisconsin on page 68 to complete the following.

1. Name the state on Wisconsin's northern border. _____

2. Name the state on Wisconsin's southern border. _____

3. Name one state on Wisconsin's western border. _____

4. Which direction(s) would you travel going . . .

   from Madison **to** Milwaukee? _____

5. **from** Green Bay **to** Eau Claire? _____

6. **from** Madison **to** La Crosse? _____

7. **from** Wausau **to** La Crosse? _____

8. **from** Kenosha **to** Eau Claire? _____

9. **from** Superior **to** Wausau? _____

10. **from** Madison **to** Green Bay? _____

11. What body of water would you cross going straight south from Appleton to Fond du Lac? _____

12. Name two of the Great Lakes that form part of Wisconsin's border. _____

13. Circle the city in which the sun will rise first.

    a. La Crosse   b. Beloit

    c. Madison   d. Wausau

14. Circle the city in which the sun will set last.

    a. Milwaukee   b. La Crosse

    c. Green Bay   d. Racine

DRINK MILK

N
W ⊕ E
S

Use with page 67.

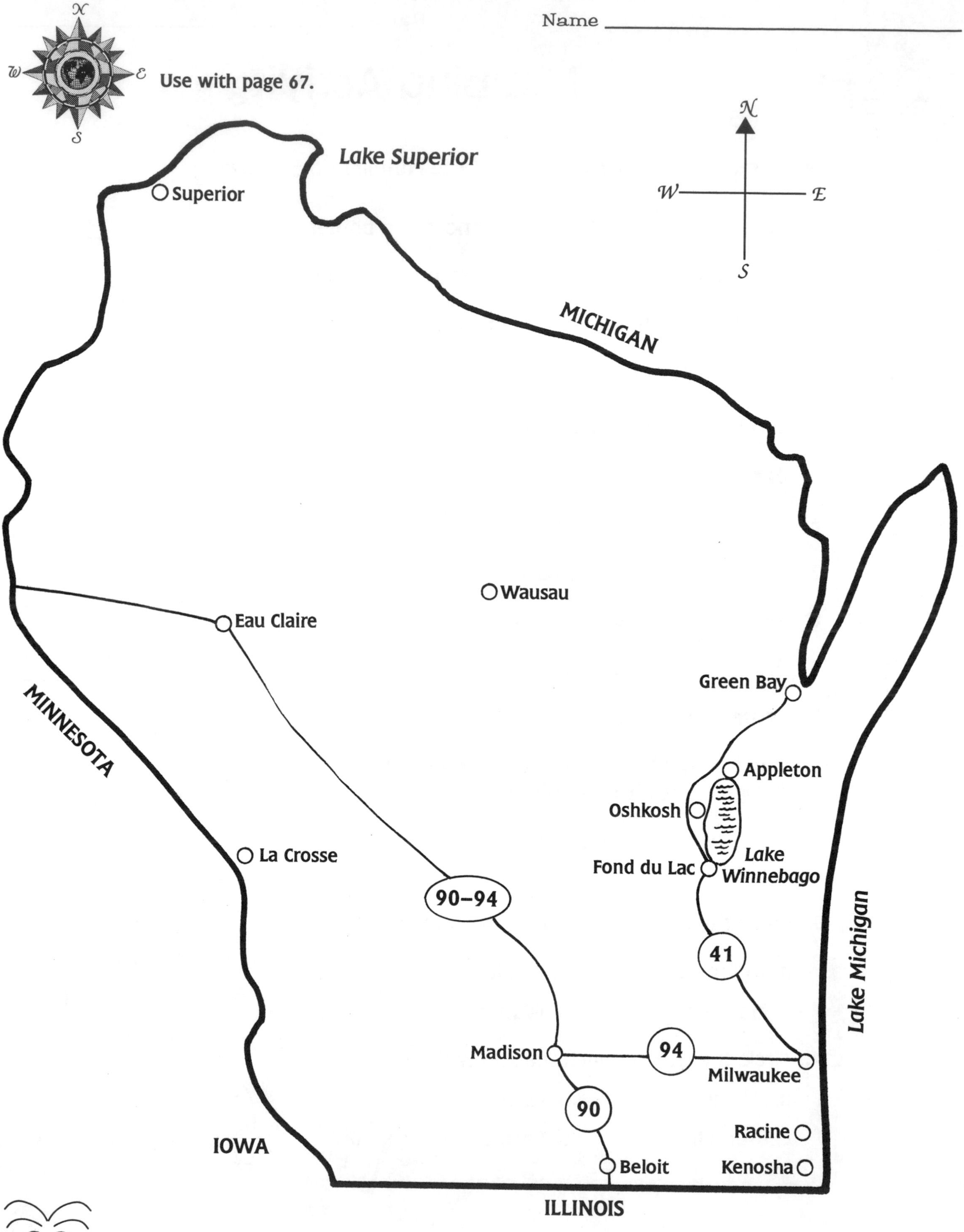

N
W ——+—— E
S

Lake Superior

○ Superior

MICHIGAN

MINNESOTA

○ Wausau

○ Eau Claire

Green Bay ○

○ Appleton

Oshkosh ○

○ La Crosse

Lake
Winnebago

Fond du Lac ○

90-94

41

Lake Michigan

Madison ○

94

Milwaukee ○

90

IOWA

Racine ○

○ Beloit

Kenosha ○

ILLINOIS

IF19311 *Social Studies Projects*

Reading Road Maps

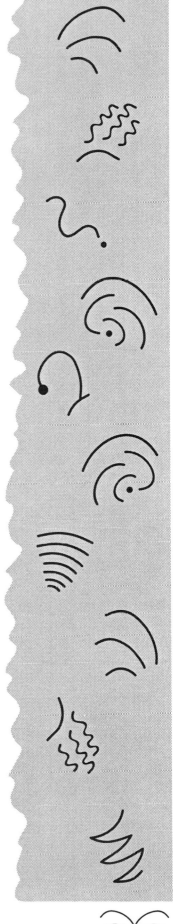

Time

One class period.

Purpose

To enable students to master the skills of reading and interpreting road maps, and calculating distance on a map.

Objectives

Students will be able to . . .

- read and interpret a road map.
- measure distance on a road map, using a scale of miles.

Vocabulary

legend
key
scale of miles

Procedures & Teaching Ideas

1. Explain to students that . . .
   - whether a person drives or not, every one should master the skill of interpreting a road map. Road maps not only tell us how to get from one place to another, but they also tell us how many miles it is from place to place; the location of highways; where campsites and lodging can be found; plus other valuable information.
   - to measure distance on a road map, you need a straight edge of some kind (ruler, protractor, note card, or sheet of paper), and you need to know the scale of miles for that particular map. Most maps print the scale of miles in one of the corners. The following formula can be used to compute scale of miles:

     Number of miles per inch multiplied by the number of inches measured from point to point.

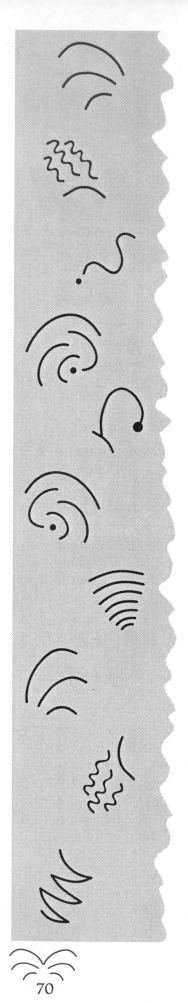

Example A: The scale of miles shows that one inch equals four miles. You measure the distance between two points and find it is two inches in length.

$$4 \text{ miles} \times 2 \text{ inches} = 8 \text{ miles}$$

Example B: The scale of miles shows that one inch equals 4.5 inches. Therefore . . .

$$4 \text{ miles} \times 4.5 \text{ miles} = 18 \text{ miles}$$

You can also measure distance without a ruler. On a sheet of paper, mark the points of the two cities. Then match the two marks to the scale of miles printed on the map. Calculate from this information to arrive at a rough estimate.

2. Explain to students that maps provide other information besides direction and mileage scales. All maps contain various symbols, colors, and codes. To understand what these mean, a person must consult the map key, or legend. The key, or legend, *explains the meanings of the symbols on the map.* It is usually located in one of the corners of the map. Assign the mapping activity, "On the Road Again . . . ," on pages 71 and 72.

3. As a final mapping activity, pass out the "Mapping Mania" worksheet on page 73, and the grading sheet on page 74.

On the Road Again . . .

Use the map on page 72 to answer the following questions.

1. What kind of road is *Highway 11*? _____

2. What city lies directly north of Eagle
   on *Highway 11*? _____

3. On the map, which city is the largest? _____

4. What kind of a road is *Highway 10*? _____

5. Give the number of the unpaved road. _____

6. What is the population **range** for Eagle? _____

7. What city is directly west of Lizard? _____

8. Which directions would you travel to go
   from Tiger to Fox? _____

9. What roads would you take to go from
   Eagle to Lion? _____

10. What roads would you take to go from
    Tiger to Deer? _____

11. Using the scale of miles, how many miles would it be if a direct line was
    drawn from . . .

    · Cat to Fox? _____

    · Lizard to Tiger? _____

    · Rabbit to Eagle? _____

12. Draw the symbol for a city with a population
    over 10,000.

13. Which roads provide the shortest
    distance from Bear to Lion? _____

14. At what city do *Highway 11* and
    Highway 12 intersect? _____

15. Name two roads that lead from
    Cat to Deer. _____

16. What direction would you travel to go
    from Deer to Hawk? _____

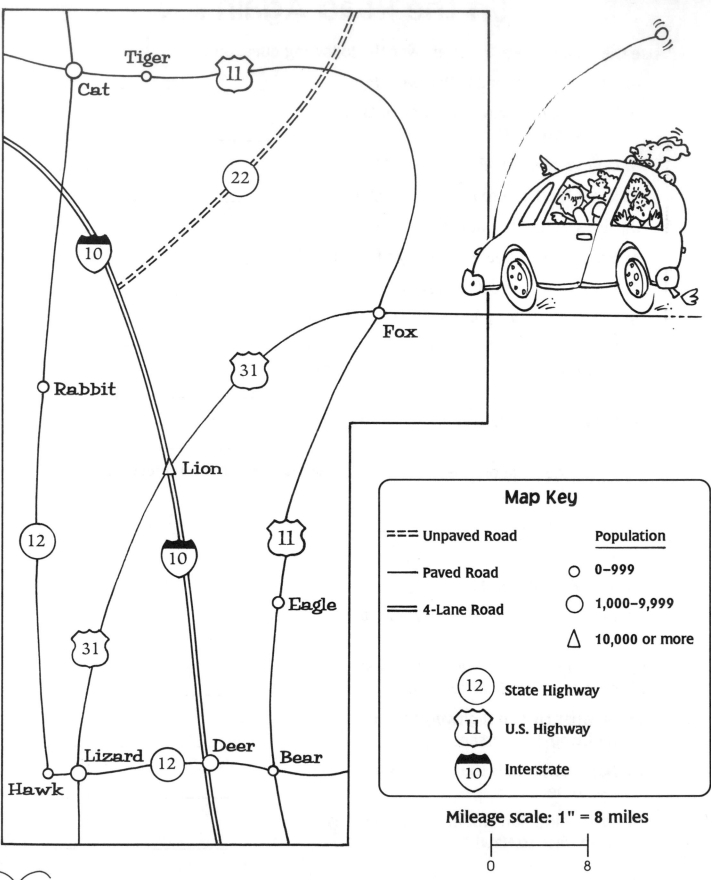

Map Key

=== Unpaved Road

— Paved Road

═══ 4-Lane Road

Population

○ 0–999

◯ 1,000–9,999

△ 10,000 or more

⑫ State Highway

⑪ U.S. Highway

⑩ Interstate

Mileage scale: 1" = 8 miles

0   8

© Instructional Fair • TS Denison   IF19311 *Social Studies Projects*

Mapping Mania

Having reviewed lessons on direction, scale of miles, and reading road maps, you should be able to draw your own map. Read the directions below and have fun creating your own map masterpiece.

Congratulations!

You have just won the largest prize ever awarded by Cublisher's Plearinghouse: $15,000,000. Our prize patrol vehicle will arrive in your school's parking lot at 3:40 in the afternoon on Friday to pick up a map directing our van to your house. Since our van driver is unfamiliar with your area, you will need to make a very detailed and accurate map, showing the route from school to your home. You must include the following information on your map:

_____ compass rose

_____ key or legend

_____ street names

_____ a scale of miles

_____ your home and address clearly marked

_____ landmarks or major attractions

_____ your name

_____ at least one paragraph with a verbal explanation of the directions

As you include each item on your map, check it off in the list above. The more details you include, the more helpful it will be to our driver. Our driver will follow your directions exactly. An inaccurate map means somebody else may get your $15,000,000. Your map should be drawn on unlined paper. It should also be neat and easy to read. Feel free to use colored pencils or markers. Good luck!

Mapping Mania
Grading Sheet

Refer to the evaluation guide below after you complete your map.

	Possible Points	Score by Student	Score by Teacher
• Compass rose	10	_____	_____
• Legend	10	_____	_____
• Street names	10	_____	_____
• Landmarks	10	_____	_____
• Your home and address	10	_____	_____
• Scale of miles	10	_____	_____
• Clearly written paragraph	10	_____	_____
• Neatly drawn map	30	_____	_____
Totals:	100	_____	_____

Letter Grade: _____

Teacher Comments: _____

_____

_____

_____

_____

_____

_____

_____

Biking or Walking Trip

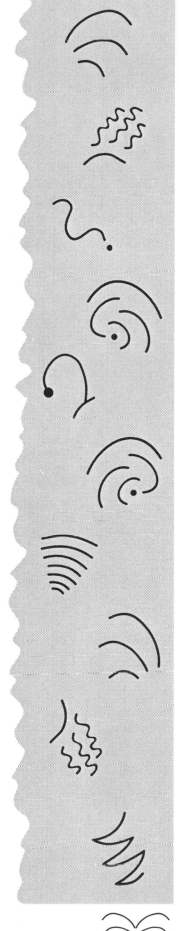

Time

One school day.

Purpose

To enable students to apply the concepts learned in the map unit to an actual situation.

Objective

Students will use maps to get from place to place in the community either by riding bicycles or by walking.

Procedures & Teaching Ideas

1. Send home a letter to parents outlining the concept of the activity. A sample can be found on page 77.

2. Have students bring lunch or preorder lunch from a restaurant. If you decide to do this, have a volunteer make all the arrangements and include an order form with the letter to parents for students to complete and return.

3. Include the "Biking Guidelines" on page 78 with the letter to parents.

4. Mark different destinations on maps so each biking and walking group will follow a different route. Each group should have different destinations, although all groups could meet at the same place for lunch. Set up the routes so each group has at least six to eight different mini-destinations. Each destination should be easy to locate using the map.

5. Organize the biking and walking groups ahead of time. A manageable group is eight or nine students with two or three volunteers per group.

6. Allow the groups to meet to plan their routes to their mini-destinations. Have three stu-

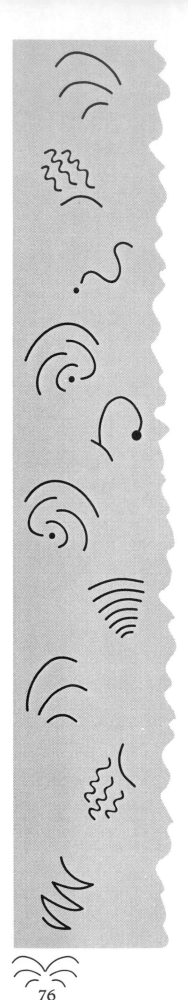

dents plan each segment and then share the proposed route with their whole group. The whole group must agree or suggest alternative routes. Avoid main roads as much as possible.

7. Give adult volunteers a copy of "Directions for Group Leaders" (page 79) on the day of the trip.

8. Give the volunteers an evaluation form to complete at the end of the trip. A sample can be found on page 80.

9. After completing the trip, discuss it with students during class the next day.

Additional Notes

• You may wish to order a school bus to take the walkers about seven or eight miles away from school and have students walk from that point back to school.

• Plan the trips to areas with which students aren't totally familiar. If they know the area well, they might not need to use the maps.

Biking/Walking Trip

Dear Parent/Guardian,

Event   On _____ our class will be participating in a
              Day/Date
              biking/walking activity that will focus on map reading and direction skills.
              The plan calls for those students who are able and willing to bike to take a
              twenty- to twenty-five-mile bike trip with teachers and parent volunteers.
              If a student does not have a bike, we will make arrangements to get
              him/her one so he/she can join us. Those who do not wish to bike will go
              on a seven- to nine-mile walking trip with teachers and parent volunteers.
              A teacher will drive to supervise the entire trip, to bring lunch to the lunch
              locations, and to assist those in need of help. Students will be given vari-
              ous destinations. Using maps of the area, each group will plan a route to
              reach each destination, avoiding busy streets as much as possible.

Volunteers   Parent volunteers are needed to help lead and direct both the walking
              groups and biking groups. I will need **at least** _____ volunteers for this
              trip.

Permission   Return the permission slip below by _____ .
                                                    Day/Date

              Direct any questions to: _____ .
                                        Teacher's Name

              Our rain date is tentatively set for _____ .
                                                  Day/Date

- -

Please Check   _____   My child will walk to take part in this activity.
Appropriate
Categories   _____   I volunteer to help lead a walking group.

                      _____   I volunteer to help lead a biking group.

                      _____   I volunteer to help lead either a biking or walking group.

                      _____   My child needs a bicycle.

_____   _____
Student's Name   Parent/Guardian Signature

Biking Guidelines

• Be sure your bike is in good working order. This includes having the tires properly inflated; the gears and brakes in good working order; and a chain which works properly. Mountain bikes and touring ten-, twelve-, and twenty-one-speed bikes are acceptable. Dirt bikes are not allowed.

• You must wear a helmet.

• Dress appropriately. Consider the weather when dressing for the trip. You can always take off a sweatshirt or jacket if you get too warm.

• Bring a few dollars along. This might be used for an emergency phone call or a refreshment stop along the way. Lunch will be at _____ and will be ordered in advance and prepaid. Adult volunteers may also preorder lunch, or bring a sack lunch if they prefer.

• A safety system is in place to avoid any member of the group getting lost. The school phone number will be on the students' maps.

• Walkmans and other electronic equipment will not be allowed.

• Be advised that there are many stops along the route where students will have time to rest.

• Each group will determine the exact route to their destination on the day of the trip.

• Those who are in need of a bike should let me know immediately.

Directions for Group Leaders

In your packet, you will find the following items:

- maps

- your group destinations

- lunch information

- Read the master list to find out information about specific needs students in your group may have. Some students may have to take medication; others are allergic to certain things; some need inhalers, and so on. Be sure you know the needs of the students in your group.

- Pass out the maps to the students assigned to your group.

- Announce the first destination to your group. You may advise the group, but in no way should you tell the group what to do. If the group makes a wrong turn or goes the wrong direction, let them. After a few blocks, ask the group to use the map to check their progress.

- Avoid main streets as much as possible. Also, cutting through private property is not allowed.

- Take attendance frequently throughout the trip.

- Please keep all members of your group in sight at all times. Adults at the front of the group should be able to see the adults at the back of the group.

- Should you need to contact the school, the phone number is _____ .
  Ask for _____ .
  Name of contact person

- Make sure students are back at school no later than _____ .
  Time

Thanks for your help! Without it, this activity
would not have been possible.

Evaluation

Dear Volunteer,

In completing this evaluation, please keep in mind the goals of the biking/walking trip:

- Students demonstrated a reasonable ability to read maps.
- Students successfully navigated from one destination to another.
- Students cooperated with one another.

Please answer the following questions by circling the most appropriate response based on your experiences and observations today.

1. How well were the students able to read the maps?

    Very Well   Adequately   Poorly

2. How well were the students able to follow the map directions?

    Very Well   Adequately   Poorly

3. Did your group get lost?   Yes   No   If yes, please explain.

    _____

    _____

4. Did your group go the wrong way at any time?   Yes   No

    If yes, please explain. _____

    _____

    _____

5. How well did the group work as a unit?

    Very Well   Adequately   Poorly

6. Do you feel this experience helped students apply the map skills they have learned?

    Yes–Excellent Experience   Yes–Average Experience

    No–Poor Experience

7. How well did the "Directions for Group Leaders" help you in leading your group?

    Very Well   Adequately   Poorly

8. Rate the effectiveness of this experience in reaching the stated goals.

    Very effective   Somewhat effective   Not at all effective

    Leader Comments: _____

    _____

    _____

Notes

_____
_____
_____
_____
_____
_____
_____
_____
_____
_____
_____
_____
_____
_____
_____
_____
_____
_____
_____
_____
_____
_____
_____
_____

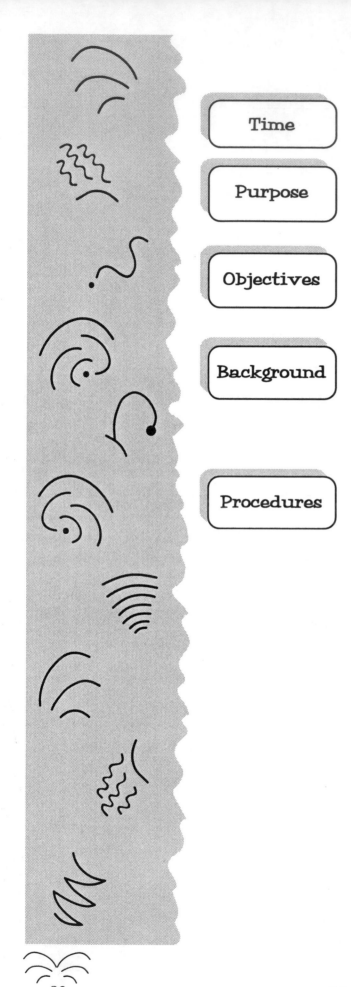

Newspaper Project

Time

Two weeks.

Purpose

To enable students to become familiar with the elements of, and the process of creating a newspaper.

Objectives

Students will be able to . . .
- create their own historical newspaper.
- identify the elements of a newspaper.

Background

Students will create a newspaper reflecting significant components of an historical period. Although the activity presented focuses on the American Revolution, the framework could be used for any given period in history.

Procedures

Have students create their own newspaper. Each newspaper will include . . .
- three articles summarizing events (social, political, economic) that happened during the time period. Each article should have a title.
- one letter to the editor stating one's opinion about a major event during the time period.
- two pictures or drawings about major events happening during the time period.
- a small crossword puzzle related to entertainment of the time period.
- a map showing weather conditions in a given region. Be sure to include a weather forecast for a particular location.
- one political cartoon.

The above requirements are minimums. Encourage students to add other elements. These may include an entertainment section, book review section, sports section, classified ads, fashion section, obituaries, and lifestyle section. Remind students to keep the articles appropriate to and factually accurate for the time period.

Historical newspaper

Assignment

Try your hand at producing a historical newspaper reflecting the time period of the American Revolution. It must represent as much of the culture as possible. Although you or your teacher may decide on a different period of time, the elements of this activity will remain the same.

Use a textbook, primary source books, and encyclopedias as resource materials.

Part of the work for this project will be done in class. Some homework will be necessary for its completion. The procedure for this project is to **write** your articles on notebook paper or on a computer, **proofread** them, and then **"print"** your articles.

Use the Writer's Guide on page 84 to evaluate your work.

Criteria

- Usual newspaper format. (Page must be divided into columns. Must be neatly done, article by article.)
- Articles will be cut out and mounted on legal- or ledger-size paper.
- Articles are to be keyed on the computer or hand-printed in black ink.
- Work must be free of mechanical errors. **Proofread**.
- Use a ruler, if applicable, for comic strips and political cartoons.
- All printing must be legible.

Required Elements

Your newspaper must contain . . .

- a masthead—name, date, city of publication, and cost.
- three articles summarizing events (social, political, economic) that happened during this time period. Each article should have a title.
- one "letter to the editor" stating your opinion about a major event taking place during this time.
- two pictures or drawings about major events happening during this time.
- one political cartoon.
- a small crossword puzzle.
- a map showing weather conditions in a given region. Be sure to include a weather forecast for a particular location.

Optional Elements

- Display Ad
- Sports Section
- Financial Section
- Obituaries
- Classified Ads
- Entertainment Section
- Comic Strip
- Other

Historical Newspaper Writer's Guide

	Possible Points	Score by Student	Score by Teacher
Masthead—Name: _____			
Date: _____			
City of Publication: _____			
Cost: _____			
Three Articles Summarizing Events	30	_____	_____
One "Letter to the Editor"	10	_____	_____
Two Pictures or Drawings of Major Events ..	20	_____	_____
Weather Report with Map	5	_____	_____
Crossword Puzzle (10-word min.)	5	_____	_____
One Political Cartoon	10	_____	_____
Mechanics	10	_____	_____
Layout	10	_____	_____
Totals		_____	_____

Optional Elements

	Possible Points	Score by Student	Score by Teacher
Entertainment Section	5	_____	_____
Sports Section	5	_____	_____
Financial Section	5	_____	_____
Display Ad (with 4" x 5" picture)....................	5	_____	_____
Classified Ads (5)	5	_____	_____
Obituaries	5	_____	_____
Comic Strip	5	_____	_____
Other	5	_____	_____
Totals			

© Instructional Fair • TS Denison   IF19311 *Social Studies Projects*

Travel Project

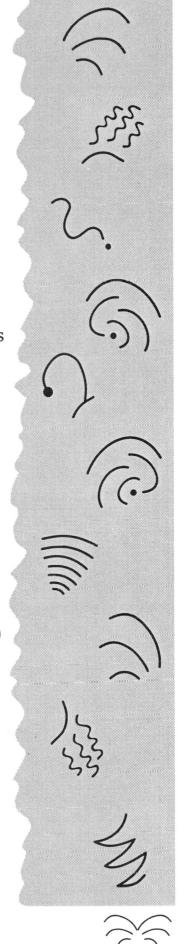

Time

Six to eight weeks.

Purpose

To enable students to understand the depths of planning involved when taking a trip, especially when traveling abroad.

Objectives

Students will be able to . . .
- identify elements that make for an enjoyable trip.
- familiarize themselves with passports, customs declarations, etc.

Background

In a geography or similar course in which students are introduced to different countries and cultures, students can plan a trip to some of the places they studied about. This project might be used toward the end of such a course. While the activity is written for a world history, geography, or international cultures class, it could easily be adapted to fit other types of social studies classes.

Procedures

1. Send a letter to students and parents explaining the project. (See sample letter on page 87.)
   - Suggest that students visit a travel agency to collect brochures, maps, and other information appropriate for the trip they are planning.
2. Explain all elements of the project as outlined below.
   - Have students collect appropriate maps from travel agencies for the trip they are planning.
   - Have students collect pictures (magazine and travel catalog pictures, or personal photos) to show highlights of their trip.

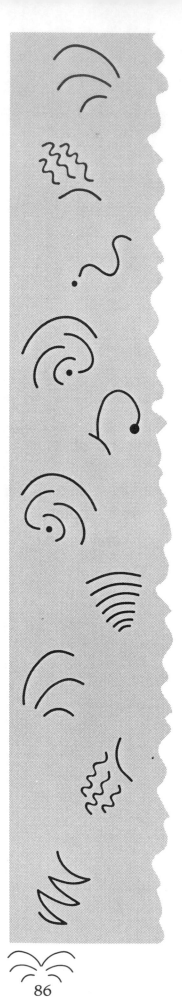

- Students will provide a written account of each country visited. Further details will be available on the student handout, "Travel Project Guidelines," on page 88.

- Give students a time line with due dates for each step. They are to fill in this information on the "Travel Project Guidelines" (page 88). Offering a choice of due dates before and after a vacation break reduces student and parent complaints!

- Have students organize their projects according to an itinerary.

- Have students use a computer or write neatly in ink for their projects.

- All reports should be placed in a three-ring binder or folder in which papers can be fastened.

- Provide students with copies of the "Project Evaluation Sheet" (page 89) that explains the grading process.

- Provide students with copies of the "Passport Application Form" (page 90) and the "Customs Declaration Form" (page 91) to fill out and include with their projects.

Dear Parent/Guardian,

    Today in social studies I outlined a detailed activity that will take students approximately 3 to 4 weeks to complete. I want to share this project with you.

    The project involves planning a trip to a foreign country. The student will provide a detailed description of the trip he/she has taken, plans to take, or would like to take to some nation(s) outside the United States. This project will include maps, pictures, passport application, and customs declaration forms. The student will provide a written summary of tourist attractions, hotel accommodations, and restaurants visited, along with other interesting highlights.

The project will count for _____% of this quarter's grade in social studies.

The project was outlined for the class on _____ and is due
Date

between _____ and _____ .
Date   Date
Direct any questions you may have to me.

Sincerely,

_____

- -

I am aware of the social studies project and will do my best to see that my son or daughter completes the project on time.

_____
        Parent/Guardian Signature

Name _____

Travel Project Guidelines

- Visit a travel agent to collect brochures, maps, and other information to complete your travel project. If possible, draw your travel route on one of your maps.

- Use pictures from magazines and travel brochures or, if available, your own personal photos to show highlights of your trip.

- Provide a written account of each country visited. Details are important here. Describe where you went; what you did and saw; some of the places where you ate and stayed; plus other interesting highlights of your trip. Writing can be narrative or written in the first person. "First person" includes letters or notes written to family or friends or "Dear Diary" accounts.

- Organize your project according to an itinerary (countries visited).

- Use a computer or write neatly by hand. Use only one side of the paper. Double-space if a computer is used.

- All reports should be in either a three-ring binder or a folder in which you can fasten the papers.

- Since there is only a limited supply of resources available at school for your use, it is very important that you visit a travel agency for certain resources to ensure the success of your project.

- To help you complete your travel project, the project has been divided into small segments with different due dates for each segment. By each date indicated below, you should have completed the following:

_____ Chosen your country(ies) and begun collecting
    Date   your materials.

_____ Finished collecting materials and locating
    Date   resources; begun research.

_____ Completed research; cut out pictures; and written
    Date   rough draft.

_____ Revised rough draft; filled out passport application.
    Date

_____ Completed customs declaration; written final copy.
    Date

_____ Proofread project; made necessary revisions; turned
    Date   in project.

© Instructional Fair • TS Denison   IF19311 *Social Studies Projects*

Travel Project Evaluation Sheet

Please complete the following evaluation guide after you complete your project.

	Possible Points	Score by Student	Score by Teacher
Organization			
Table of Contents	5	_____	_____
Neatly Assembled	5	_____	_____
Pictures neatly cut out	5	_____	_____
Mechanics			
Grammar	5	_____	_____
Spelling	5	_____	_____
Punctuation	5	_____	_____
Content			
Maps	10	_____	_____
Pictures	10	_____	_____
Details	10	_____	_____
Accuracy	10	_____	_____
Informative Content	10	_____	_____
Passport Application Form	10	_____	_____
Customs Declaration Form	10	_____	_____
Totals:	100	_____	_____

Teacher Comments:

_____

_____

Passport Application Form

UNITED STATES DEPARTMENT OF STATE

APPLICATION FOR ☐ PASSPORT ☐ REGISTRATION

SEE INSTRUCTIONS—TYPE OR PRINT IN INK

1. NAME   FIRST NAME _____   MIDDLE NAME _____

   LAST NAME _____

2. MAILING ADDRESS _____

   STREET _____

   CITY, STATE, ZIP CODE _____

   COUNTRY _____   IN CARE OF _____

☐ 5 Yr. ☐ 10 Yr.

R   D   O   DP

End. # _____

Issue Date _____

Exp. _____

3. SEX   Male   Female

4. PLACE OF BIRTH City, State or Province, Country _____

5. DATE OF BIRTH   ☐☐ Mo.   ☐☐ Day   ☐☐ Year

6. SOCIAL SECURITY NUMBER | | | | | | |

7. HEIGHT   Feet | Inches

8. COLOR OF HAIR _____

9. COLOR OF EYES _____

10. (Area Code) HOME PHONE _____

11. (Area Code) BUSINESS PHONE _____

12. PERMANENT ADDRESS (Street, City, State, ZIP Code) _____

13. OCCUPATION _____

14. FATHER'S NAME _____   BIRTHPLACE _____   BIRTH DATE _____   U.S. CITIZEN ☐ YES ☐ NO

15. MOTHER'S MAIDEN NAME _____   BIRTHPLACE _____   BIRTH DATE _____   U.S. CITIZEN ☐ YES ☐ NO

16. TRAVEL PLANS (Not Mandatory)   COUNTRIES   DEPARTURE DATE _____   LENGTH OF STAY _____

17. HAVE YOU EVER BEEN ISSUED A U.S. PASSPORT? ☐ YES ☐ NO   IF YES, SUBMIT PASSPORT IF AVAILABLE ☐ Submitted

IF UNABLE TO SUBMIT MOST RECENT PASSPORT, STATE ITS DISPOSITION: COMPLETE NEXT LINE

NAME IN WHICH ISSUED _____   PASSPORT NUMBER | | | | | | | ISSUE DATE (Mo., Day, Yr.) ☐☐☐☐   DISPOSITION

SUBMIT TWO RECENT IDENTICAL PHOTOS

FROM 1" TO 1-3/8"

FOLD

18. HAVE YOU EVER BEEN MARRIED? ☐ YES ☐ NO   DATE OF MOST RECENT MARRIAGE ☐☐ Mo. ☐☐ Day ☐☐ Year

WIDOWED/DIVORCED? ☐ YES ☐ NO   IF YES, GIVE DATE ☐☐ Mo. ☐☐ Day ☐☐ Year

SPOUSE'S BIRTH NAME _____   SPOUSE'S BIRTHPLACE _____

19. IN CASE OF EMERGENCY, NOTIFY (Person Not Traveling With You)   RELATIONSHIP _____
   (Not Mandatory)

FULL NAME _____   (Area Code) PHONE NUMBER | | | | | | |

ADDRESS _____

20. TO BE COMPLETED BY AN APPLICANT WHO BECAME A CITIZEN THROUGH NATURALIZATION

I IMMIGRATED TO THE U.S. (Month, Year) ☐☐   I RESIDED CONTINUOUSLY IN THE U.S. From (Mo., Yr.) ☐☐ To (Mo., Yr.) ☐☐   DATE NATURALIZED (Mo. Day, Yr.) ☐☐☐☐

PLACE _____

21. DO NOT SIGN APPLICATION UNTIL REQUESTED TO DO SO BY PERSON ADMINISTERING OATH

I have not, since acquiring United States citizenship, performed any of the acts listed under "Acts or Conditions" on the reverse of this application form (unless explanatory statement is attached). I solemnly swear (or affirm) that the statements made on this application are true and the photograph attached is a true likeness of me.

Subscribed and sworn to (affirmed) before me   (SEAL)

☐☐☐ Month Day Year

☐ Clerk of Court or
☐ PASSPORT Agent
☐ Postal Employee
☐ (Vice) Consul USA At _____

X _____
(Sign in presence of person authorized to accept application)

_____
(Signature of person authorized to accept application)

22. APPLICANT'S IDENTIFYING DOCUMENTS   ☐ PASSPORT ☐ DRIVER'S LICENSE ☐ OTHER (Specify)   No. _____

ISSUE DATE ☐☐☐ Month Day Year   EXPIRATION DATE ☐☐☐ Month Day Year   ISSUED IN THE NAME OF _____

23. FOR ISSUING OFFICE USE ONLY (Applicant's evidence of citizenship)

☐ Birth Cert.   SR   CR   City _____   Filed/Issued: _____

☐ Passport

☐ Report of Birth   Bearer's Name: _____

☐ Naturalization/Citizenship Cert.   No. _____

☐ Other:

☐ Seen & Returned

APPLICATION APPROVAL

Examiner Name

Office, Date

© Instructional Fair • TS Denison   IF19311 *Social Studies Projects*

Customs Declaration Form

Back

WARNING

The smuggling or unlawful importation of controlled substances regardless of amount is a violation of U.S. law.

Accuracy of your declaration may be verified through questioning and physical search.

AGRICULTURAL PRODUCTS

To prevent the entry of dangerous agricultural pests the following are restricted: Fruits, vegetables, plants, plant products, soil, meats, meat products, birds, snails, and other live animals or animal products. Failure to declare all such items to a Customs/Agriculture Officer can result in fines or other penalties.

CURRENCY AND MONETARY INSTRUMENTS

The transportation of currency or monetary instruments, regardless of amount, is legal; however, if you take out of or bring into (or are about to take out of or bring into) the United States more than $10,000 (U.S. or foreign equivalent, or a combination of the two) in coin, currency, travelers checks or bearer instruments such as money orders, checks, stocks or bonds, you are required by law to file a report on a Form 4790 with the U.S. Customs Service. If you have someone else carry the currency or instruments for you, you must also file the report. FAILURE TO FILE THE REQUIRED REPORT OR FALSE STATEMENTS ON THE REPORT MAY LEAD TO SEIZURE OF THE CURRENCY OR INSTRUMENTS AND TO CIVIL PENALTIES AND/OR CRIMINAL PROSECUTION.

MERCHANDISE

IN ITEM 11, **U.S. residents** must declare the total value of ALL articles acquired abroad (whether new or used, whether dutiable or not, and whether obtained by purchase, as a gift, or otherwise), including those purchases made in DUTY FREE stores in the U.S. or abroad, which are in their or their family's possession at the time of arrival. **Visitors** must declare in Item 11 the total value of all gifts and commercial items, including samples they are bringing with them.

The amount of duty to be paid will be determined by a Customs officer. U.S. residents are normally entitled to a duty free exemption of $400 on those items accompanying them; non-residents are normally entitled to an exemption of $100. Both residents and non-residents will normally be required to pay a flat 10% rate of duty on the first $1,000 above their exemptions.

If the value of goods declared in Item 11 EXCEEDS $1,400 PER PERSON, then list ALL articles below and show price paid in U.S. dollars or, for gifts, fair retail value. If additional space is needed, continue on another Customs Form 6059B.

DESCRIPTION OF ARTICLES	PRICE	CUSTOMS USE
TOTAL		

IF YOU HAVE ANY QUESTIONS ABOUT WHAT MUST BE REPORTED OR DECLARED ASK A CUSTOMS OFFICER.

I have read the above statements and have made a truthful declaration.

....
Signature   DATE (Day/Month/Year)

★ U.S.G.P.O.: 1993 748-014   Form 6059B (092089)

Front

WELCOME TO THE UNITED STATES

DEPARTMENT OF THE TREASURY   FORM APPROVED
UNITED STATES CUSTOMS SERVICE   OMB NO. 1515-0041

CUSTOMS DECLARATION

19 CFR 122.27,148.12, 148.13, 148.110, 148.111

Each arriving traveler or head of family must provide the following information (only ONE written declaration per family is required):

1. Name: _____ _____ _____
          Last   First   Middle Initial

2. Date of Birth: ___ / ___ / ___
                  Day Month Year

3. Airline/Flight _____

4. Number of family members traveling with you _____

5. U.S. Address: _____
   City: _____ State _____

6. I am a U.S. Citizen   YES ☐   NO ☐
   If No,
   Country: _____

7. I reside permanently in the U.S.   YES ☐   NO ☐
   If No,
   Expected Length of Stay: _____

8. The purpose of my trip is or was   ☐ BUSINESS   ☐ PLEASURE

9. I am/we are bringing fruits, plants, meats, food,   YES ☐   NO ☐
   soil, birds, snails, other live animals, farm
   products, or I/we have been on a farm or ranch
   outside the U.S.

10. I am/we are carrying currency or monetary   YES ☐   NO ☐
    instruments over $10,000 U.S. or foreign
    equivalent.

11. The total value of all goods I/we purchased or
    acquired abroad and am/are bringing to the U.S.
    is (see instructions under Merchandise on reverse
    side): $ _____ US Dollars

▶ **MOST MAJOR CREDIT CARDS ACCEPTED.**

SIGN ON REVERSE SIDE AFTER YOU READ WARNING.
(Do not write below this line.)

INSPECTOR'S NAME	STAMP AREA
BADGE NO.	

Paperwork Reduction Act Notice: The Paperwork Reduction Act of 1980 says we must tell you why we are collecting this information, how we will use it and whether you have to give it to us. We ask for this information to carry out the Customs, Agriculture, and Currency laws of the United States. We need it to ensure the that travelers are complying with these laws and to allow us to figure and collect the right amounts of duties and taxes. Your response is mandatory.

Statement required by 5 CFR 1320.21: The estimated average burden associated with this collection of information is 3 minutes per respondent or recordkeeper depending on individual circumstances. Comments concerning the accuracy of this burden estimate and suggestions for reducing this burden should be directed to U.S. Customs Service, Paperwork Management Branch, Washington, DC 20229, and to the Office of Management and Budget, Paperwork Reduction Project (1515-0041). Washington, DC 2C0503.

Customs Form 6059B (C92089)

Constitution Project

Time

5–10 class periods.

Purpose

To enable students to appreciate the effort involved in writing a document that is workable.

Objective

Students will be able to organize and develop a school constitution.

Background

After studying the U.S. Constitution, have the students develop a constitution for their own school. Students could work individually, but working in pairs or in groups provides a cooperative learning experience, and students will be less intimidated by the project.

Procedures

Explain to students that they will be writing a constitution for the student body at their school. The document is very important, as it will serve as an operating guide for all students, present and future.

Constitution Project

Your responsibility is an awesome one. Developing a set of rules and regulations for your school is no easy task. It will be necessary to consider the needs of all students. You have been selected for this task because you have demonstrated an ability to make wise decisions! Good luck as you take on this monumental responsibility. We will see you at the Constitutional Convention in two weeks.

Your constitution will contain, at a minimum, the following elements:

A. Preamble—introduction which states the purpose for the constitution.

B. Article I—Legislative branch or lawmaking body.

Be sure to state . . .

- the name of the lawmaking body.

- the qualifications for members of the lawmaking body.

- how a person can be elected to it.

- the length of the term of office.

- the procedures for passing a law.

- the powers of the lawmaking body. Be sure to specify the areas the laws will address.

C. Article II—Judicial branch or court system.

Be sure to state . . .

- how cases will be tried (a judge, a jury, or combination judge/jury).

- the qualifications for judges.

- how a person can become a judge.

- how a jury (if you have one) will be chosen.

- five examples of punishments a person could receive for breaking a law.

D. Student Bill of Rights—guaranteed student rights. List at least five and no more than ten.

E. Amendment Process
Outline the specific process for changing your constitution.

Constitution Evaluation Sheet

Please refer to the following guide as you complete your project.

	Possible Points	Score by Student	Score by Teacher
Required Elements			
Preamble	15	_____	_____
Legislative Branch	15	_____	_____
Judicial Branch	15	_____	_____
Bill of Rights	15	_____	_____
Amendment Process	15	_____	_____
Mechanics			
Grammar	5	_____	_____
Spelling	5	_____	_____
Punctuation	5	_____	_____
Organization			
Neatly Assembled	10	_____	_____
Totals	100	_____	_____

Letter Grade _____

Teacher Comments: _____

_____

_____

Page 12

Here are some suggested answers for page 12. Students and teachers may think of other possibilities not listed here.

Event A

- One could buy clothing and give up the concert tickets and CDs.
- One could buy the concert tickets and CDs and give up the clothing.
- One could buy the CDs and some clothing and give up the concert tickets and some clothing items.
- One could buy the concert tickets and some clothing and give up the CDs and some clothing items.

Event B

- The sorters could help sell stamps. Then, the mail carriers would have to sort, thus delaying delivery. Customers might become angry and file complaints. Business could be lost if people turned to UPS or Federal Express.
- The sorters could sell stamps. They would then have to work overtime to catch up on the sorting. This would be expensive. Mail service could be delayed, and business could be lost if people turn to other carriers.
- The sorters could keep on sorting. However, long lines would form, resulting in people becoming impatient or angry and complaining of poor customer service. Some business could be lost if people turned to other sources.
- Postal managers could come forward to sell. However, their managerial duties would be neglected.

Event C

- If you called in the non-city workers it would be expensive, and it could cause dissent among city workers. It could cause problems in future contract negotiations. Taxes could rise as a result.
- You could use only the city workers. However, citizens may become angry as service will not be timely. Property may be damaged, whereas bringing in non-city employees could prevent some of these losses. There will likely be overtime costs; as mayor, you could lose the next election as a result.
- You could send a minimum number of workers to each water main break. However, the workers may not be able to deal with the breaks in a timely fashion because of the labor shortage. This could lead to a lot of unhappy people. You could be defeated in the next election because people would perceive the situation as poor service and poor management.
- You could repair the break of highest priority first. This will make people at the end of the list angry and feeling unimportant.

Page 21

1. How many CCs could you buy if the price of each was four dollars? <u>5</u>
2. If the price of each was five dollars? <u>4</u>
3. If the price of each was ten dollars? <u>2</u>
4. If the price of each was twenty dollars? <u>1</u>
5. What do you notice about demand as the price increases?

   Demand goes down as the price increases.

Page 21 (cont.)

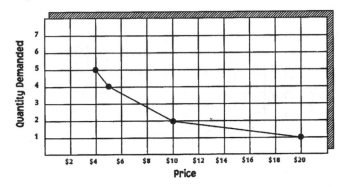

Page 22

Price Per Slice	Profit Per Pizza	Projected Number Sold	Total Profit
.40	-80¢	0	-0-
.50	-0-	50	-0-
.60	80¢	30	$40.00
.75	$2.00	40	$80.00
.80	$2.40	35	$84.00
.90	$3.20	30	$96.00
$1.00	$4.00	20	$80.00

1. At what point does the class break even? <u>At 50¢ per slice.</u>
2. For what price should the class sell the pizzas? Explain. <u>At 90¢ per slice. The largest profit should be realized at this price.</u>
3. How many pizzas should they bake? Explain. <u>30—because the higher the price, the fewer that will be sold. However, there is also less chance of waste.</u>
4. How many days will it take to earn $600 for the trip? <u>7 days</u>

Page 24

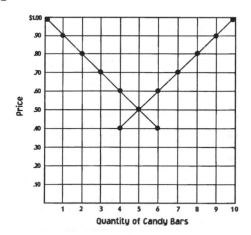

The graph indicates that five candy bars should be supplied at a cost of 50¢ each.

Page 25

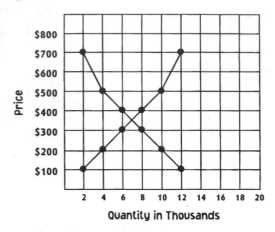

Quantity in Thousands

The graph illustrates that about 7,000 lawn mowers should be produced and sold at a price of about $350.00 each.

Page 36

Here is an explanation of the stock activity chart.

1. You will want to stress that all groups start with $1,000 cash and no stock. After you announce the initial stock price of $20, students decide whether to purchase some stock or keep their cash. If they were to purchase 20 shares, it would cost $400. They would have $600 in cash and $400 worth of stock, for total assests of $1,000.

2. After you read the first event, students will decide whether or not to purchase stock. After they make their decision, you announce the new price of $40 per share. If they had decided to sell 10 shares, it would bring $400 in cash. So, they now will have $1,000 in cash, plus the 10 shares from their initial purchase worth $400, for total assests of $1,400. **See the chart below for possible completion; it is more than likely all groups will vary considerably.**

3. Students will continue to fill in all calculations on the chart based on the information provided by the teacher.

Event	Transaction	Number of Shares Bought or Sold	Price Per Share	Transaction Amount	Total Shares Owned	Value of Shares Owned	Cash in the Bank	Total Assets
Beginning Balance	None	0	$20	$0	0	$0	$1,000	$1,000
Initial Investment	Buy	20	$20	$400	20	$400	$600	$1,000
1	Sell	10	$40	$400	10	$400	$1,000	$1,400
2	Hold	0	$16	$0	10	$150	$1,000	$1,150
3	Buy	30	$5	$150	40	$200	$850	$1,050
4	Buy	10	$15	$150	50	$750	$700	$1,450
5	Hold	0	$8	$0	50	$400	$700	$1,100
6	Sell	20	$25	$500	30	$750	$1,200	$1,950
7	Sell	20	$35	$700	10	$350	$1,900	$2,250

Page 67

1. Michigan
2. Illinois
3. Minnesota/Iowa
4. East
5. West
6. Northwest
7. Southwest
8. Northwest
9. Southeast
10. Northeast
11. Lake Winnebago
12. Lakes Michigan and Superior
13. Beloit
14. La Crosse

Page 71

1. paved
2. Fox
3. Lion
4. 4-lane highway
5. 22
6. 0–999
7. Hawk
8. East, then South
9. Sugg. U.S.11 and U.S.31
10. U.S.11, U.S.12, and I10
11. Approx. 45 miles
    Approx. 65 miles
    Approx. 65 miles
12. △
13. U.S.12 and I10
14. Deer
15. Highways 11 and 12
16. West